Lex Orandi Series

The Sacrament of Anointing of the Sick

Lex Orandi Series

John D. Laurance, S.J.
Editor

The Sacrament of
Anointing of the Sick

Lizette Larson-Miller

LITURGICAL PRESS
Collegeville, Minnesota

www.litpress.org

1   2   3   4   5   6   7   8

Library of Congress Cataloging-in-Publication Data

Larson-Miller , Lizette.
    The sacrament of anointing of the sick / Lizette Larson-Miller.
        p.   cm. — (Lex orandi series)
    Summary: "Overviews, affirms, and critiques the current Roman Catholic rites for the pastoral care of the sick and engages them through contemporary theological, liturgical, pastoral, and cultural issues, focusing particularly on the sacramental heart of the rites, the anointing of the sick"—Provided by publisher.
    Includes bibliographical references and index.
    ISBN-13: 978-0-8146-2523-1 (alk. paper)
    ISBN-10: 0-8146-2523-1 (alk. paper)
    1. Church work with the sick—Catholic Church.   2. Unction.   3. Catholic Church—Doctrines.   I. Title.   II. Series.

BX2347.8.S5L37   2005
264'.02087—dc22

                                            2005004998

Contents

Preface to the *Lex Orandi* Series

T he theology of the seven sacraments prevalent in the Catholic Church through most of the second millennium interpreted those rites more as sacred objects to be *passively* received than as *active* participations in Christ's paschal mystery. And their meaning was to be derived, not from the shape of their liturgical celebration, but from the Church's official teaching, teaching typically occasioned by historical challenges to her faith. Whereas in patristic times Church writers expounded the theology of the sacraments from the rites themselves, with the later expansion of Christianity into central Europe, confidence waned that the form and enactment of the liturgy in any way *manifested* the Mystery it contained. As the *Adoro Te Devote*, a medieval hymn on the Church's use of bread in the Eucharistic Liturgy, puts it, "Seeing, tasting, touching are in Thee deceived."

In recent times, however, there has been a kind of "Copernican revolution" in sacramental theology. Not only have sacraments come to be understood as actions of God *and* the Church, the truth of the ancient adage, *lex orandi, lex credendi* (how the Church prays expresses what she believes), has also been seen in a new light. Theologians have come to realize that if all Church dogma is rooted ultimately in her faith-experience of God, so, too, must her understanding of the sacraments derive from her experience of their liturgical celebration. Sacraments, too, must *manifest* the Mystery they contain. Consequently, in the tradition of ancient mystagogies, "liturgical theology"—that is, God's word ("first theology") to the Church through her worship—has come to be understood, along with official Church teaching, as an indispensable source for sacramental theology. And sacramental theology itself has returned to its proper place within a larger "theology of liturgy." The works of theologians such as Guardini, Casel, Rahner, Schmemann, Kilmartin, and Chauvet mark various stages in this historical development.

Although much has been written on the role of the celebrating Church, up until now no set of studies on all seven sacraments that we know of has attempted to exegete their meaning primarily from their typical celebrations. The aim of this present series, then, is precisely to investigate the sacraments as liturgical events in order to discover in them the faith understanding of Christian life of which they are both the source and the summit (SC 10).

However, since the theology of liturgy is but one part of the whole of systematic theology, liturgical events can be adequately interpreted as witnesses to the Church's faith only in light of the other ways she experiences God's word. Accordingly, individual volumes in this series analyze typical experiences of the rites they cover against the background of the rest of the Church's traditional life and teaching, and they do so guided by the unique synthesis of that tradition that each author, as theologian, brings to the work. To do anything less would be to fail in the task of theology. On occasion, then, authors will offer their own critique, whether of the rites themselves or of how they have experienced their celebration, doing so on the basis of other theological sources as well (including, for example, the official instructions introducing each rite).

Sacraments as liturgical *events* are not understood by most theologians today as they once were, that is, as so-called "moments of consecration" (the "This is my Body," the pouring of water " . . . in the name of the Father . . . ," etc.). Rather, similar to how Aristotle's *Poetics* envisions Greek tragedies, sacraments are seen as events extended through time, having beginnings, middles, and ends. True, as protracted events they include indispensable high points, but separated from the whole liturgical celebration, those key moments, at least in the short run, lose much of their intelligibility and intensity and, therefore, their efficacy as well (cf. SC 14). Accordingly, volumes in this series attempt to study each sacrament as it unfolds through its total performance, discerning especially its basic structure and how various elements contribute to its overall faith meaning.

The motivating purpose of this new series on the sacraments is ultimately a pastoral one: to help foster the fuller liturgical participation called for by Vatican II, and not necessarily to "break new ground" in sacramental theology. The readership envisioned by the series, therefore, is a broad one, not confined just to liturgical experts. Individual volumes presuppose only a beginner's familiarity with Christian theology, such as that possessed by university upper-level undergraduate or master's level students.

Finally, the rites studied in this series are those of the Roman Rite of the Catholic Church in use today. As valuable as a comparison of various Christian liturgies would be, no one series can do everything. At the same time, it is hoped that efforts made here toward understanding the Roman Rite might help inspire other, more explicitly ecumenical studies of Christian liturgy.

John D. Laurance, S.J.
Marquette University

Introduction

When the Church cares for the sick, it serves Christ himself in the suffering members of his Mystical Body . . . the Church shows this solicitude not only by visiting those who are in poor health but also by raising them up through the sacrament of anointing and by nourishing them with the eucharist during their illness and when they are in danger of death.[1]

This summary, from the "Decree of the Sacred Congregation for Divine Worship" introducing Pastoral Care of the Sick, establishes the christological and ecclesiological bases for care of the sick, especially through the breadth of the care, the depth of the sacramental focus, and the continuity of that care through the dying and death of a Christian. Every sacrament of the Church is part of an extensive series of ongoing rituals and relationships, and the anointing of the sick is no exception. If anything, anointing of the sick exemplifies more than many sacramental rites this "family relationship" to a broader array of ritual patterns. Imbedded in a rich collection of prayers, rituals, and suggested scriptural texts, the anointing of the sick is part of a series of ritual interactions and texts designed to communicate the reality of the abiding presence of Christ to the sick through the ministry of members of the Christian community. Much of the emphasis in the prayers is on "raising up" the sick persons through overcoming the alienation that sick members often feel from their community and from God through acts of prayerful solidarity and compassionate presence.

The current rite *(Ordo unctionis infirmorum eorumque pastoralis curae)* was promulgated in 1972 with the English language edition for the United States approved in 1982 and promulgated in 1983. This American edition of *Pastoral Care of the Sick: Rites of Anointing and Viaticum* is often published with "other approved parts of the Roman Ritual, for example, *Rite of Funerals, Rite of Christian Initiation of Adults*"[2] and the *Rite of Penance,* which situates the sacrament of the anointing of the sick in an even wider array of textual and ritual choices for all who minister to the sick and dying.[3] The issue of how the Church accompanies and supports those who are sick throughout their journey and at each of the turning points of illness is, as Mary Collins says, "a distinctive feature of the *Ordo unctionis infirmorum eorumque pastoralis curae.*"[4] The comprehensive scope of pastoral care, extending on both sides of the issue of sacramental care for the "seriously"[5] sick is one of the hallmarks of the rite, especially when compared to its immediate predecessor, extreme unction.

It is striking that the Pastoral Care of the Sick (hereafter PCS), inclusive of all of its ritual dimensions, is the only sacramental rite with the word "pastoral" in the title. The implications are not that other rites are not pastoral, but that the concept is central in this rite in a particular way. What does "pastoral" mean in this case? If one makes reference to other liturgical documents and to secondary descriptions, a number of meanings emerge. Etymologically the word carries a fundamental sense of shepherding or leading, taking care of, watching over, "herding together."[6] That sense of care gives rise to the field of study often called "pastoral care," caring for those within one's group of responsibility, caring for those in need: "pastoral care is care for human need."[7] And whereas pastoral care focused on attentiveness to the needs of the individual person is sometimes cast as opposed to ritual, the PCS makes explicit the recognition that they are not opposed but woven together, each functioning as a vehicle of expression for the other in an efficacious synergy.[8]

Charles Gusmer, in his classic textbook on the reformed rites of anointing the sick, *And You Visited Me: Sacramental Ministry to the Sick and the Dying,*[9] reminds his readers of another dimension of the term "pastoral" by calling attention to the paragraphs in the *praenotanda,* or theological introduction, which broaden the participation of those involved in the doing of the rite, both as ministers and as recipients of the anointing: "This ministry is the common responsibility of all Christians, who should visit the sick, remember them in prayer, and celebrate the sacraments with them."[10] Gusmer sees this widening of "earlier sacramental categories" as a key element of the rite's "overall pastoral thrust,"[11] thereby pointing us to the concept of inclusivity as a central meaning. Here "pastoral ritual" means that which is flexible enough to allow more people to participate, either as ministers or as those in need of healing, and hospitable enough to include family members and friends in the Church and beyond. This is certainly consistent with the use of the term "pastoral" in documents such as Music in Catholic Worship, which gives us a third meaning for the term "pastoral." MCW uses three different judgments to determine appropriate music for liturgy: musical, liturgical, and pastoral,[12] the latter meaning that which is appropriate to a concrete situation in a particular place and time. Speaking of music in liturgy specifically, but certainly in a paradigmatic way applicable to other situations, the authors say that

> The signs of the celebration must be accepted and received as mean-
> ingful for a genuinely human faith experience for these specific wor-
> shipers. This pastoral judgment can be aided by sensitivity to the
> cultural and social characteristics of the people who make up the
> congregation: their age, culture, and education. These factors influ-
> ence the effectiveness of the liturgical signs, including music.[13]

Utilizing this understanding of pastoral is also consistent with the PCS in that its flexibility allows for application in many different situations, cultures, and circumstances, all of which support the richness of the meanings of "pastoral" in these rites.

The variety and extent of resources in PCS, together with the theological introduction, present a very different view of the rites surrounding the sick and dying than the pre-Vatican II model of extreme unction, most obviously in the extent of ritual responses mentioned above and in the repeatability of a sacramental rite for the sick rather than a single rite for the dying. The overall effect is of a reformed rite more consistent with a twentieth-century consensus in sacramental theology in which sacraments are seen as graced moments of encounter in an ongoing relationship between God and individuals and between God, the Body of Christ and individual members thereof. Sacramental encounter and relationship also imply reciprocity, even if not that of equals. Again, the reformed rite, in the introduction and in the recurring emphasis on ecclesial presence, points to the sick person as an active participant and witness to Christ in the ministry *of* the sick, not just as passive recipient of ministry *to* the sick.

Living into this rite over the last decades has allowed participants at all levels of engagement to reflect on the rituals and their intrinsic theological interpretation that say something very different than the immediate ritual predecessor. Extreme unction served as the last anointing,

part of the last rites focused on the forgiveness of sins and preparation
for death, in spite of the Council of Trent's desire to leave open the
possibility of physical healing.[14] The PCS puts in tangible form the
charge of the Second Vatican Council, which articulated the primary
reasons for the changes that would occur:

> "Extreme Unction," which may also and more properly be called
> "anointing of the sick," is not a sacrament for those only who are at
> the point of death. Hence, as soon as any one of the faithful begins to
> be in danger of death from sickness or old age, the fitting time for that
> person to receive this sacrament has certainly already arrived.[15]

This theological and ritual change is consistent with the larger liturgical and theological agenda of Vatican II in which the wisdom and practice of earlier centuries were mined and restructured to reconstruct
sacramental rites reflecting the centrality of the Paschal Mystery. At
the same time, it raises the question of what it means to restore earlier
practices in a very different time and culture. Particularly with regard
to the anointing of the sick, changes in our understandings of the
human person, of biology in general, and of developments in medicine
and in culture itself create a very different context than that of the first
millennium of Christianity in which many of these ritual practices
have their roots. In spite of this, surveys and anecdotal evidence have
reflected a widespread appreciation and acceptance of the new rite in
this country, in some places even beyond the institutional ability to respond to requests for the sacrament.[16]

Does the general acceptance of the "new rite" also imply acceptance
of its theological presuppositions? The theological introductions to each
of the post-conciliar rites provide a valuable insight into the biblical,
historical, and theological foundations of the ritual, in some cases pro-
viding a rationale for particular ritual choices and in other cases reflecting an inherited ritual pattern that determines the scope of meaning
and interpretation of why the Church does what the Church does. In
either case, liturgical and sacramental theologians advocate that the
theological introduction and the ritual should say the same thing—one
with prose, the other through people, gesture, words, things and actions.
This first theological presupposition of *lex orandi, lex credendi*,[17] that the
theological description of the rite should reflect the actual liturgical
doing of the theology, also presumes a series of integral relationships.
There must be a ritual focus on the sick individual *and* on the worship
of God and the presence of Christ as in all liturgy. There must be ritual

authenticity and integrity in the rites *and* an honest articulation of the Church's sacramental theology regarding what it means to be sick and what healing itself means. There must be a true and loving expression of care for individual members of the Church *and* the willingness to see them as witnesses to the suffering of Christ and prophets of the reign of God in our midst. There must be real prayer for real healing *and* faith that the actions of the Holy Spirit and the Church are always about ultimate health in salvation. There must be theological and ritual attentiveness to the Church's care for the sick and dying *and* the necessary articulation that this sacrament is part of the larger sacramental activity of the Church.

Out of this relational web emerge the fundamental questions that touch the sick person and all those who minister to and around sick individuals. What is the meaning of sickness? What is health and wholeness? What has this to do with Jesus Christ? What has this to do with the Church? What do we think, expect, or hope will happen in this sacramental encounter? What does this sacrament do? The theological introduction to the rite addresses a number of these questions, some of them richly and prophetically, some of them inadequately. And the rite, even with all of its flexibility, gives human expression to unanswerable mysteries, often with surprising certitude.

To explore the sacrament of the anointing of the sick in its reality, which is the liturgical rite unfolding in the event of celebration, the rite itself will be reviewed in order to listen to the structure of the liturgy and to the words and actions defined as central to the doing of this ritual. In addition, the crucial role played by the fundamental biblical text from the Letter of James in reconstructing a rite for the sick, rather than only for the dying, will be explored as both rationale and corrective to the changes in the rite. Following that outline in the first chapter, the second chapter will explore the central sacramental ideas surrounding the anointing of the sick that emerge from the three primary actions: the prayer of faith, the laying on of hands, and the anointing with blessed oil. Each of these ritual components reveals a wealth of meaning related to the overall practices of pastoral care of the sick and each allows for theological and liturgical development from the rite itself.

The remaining chapters will begin from the perspective of the *praenotanda* that addresses presuppositions and ecclesial interpretations surrounding the sick. No liturgy begins as a blank slate, free of pre-existing theological definitions, and the ritual and pastoral care of the sick is particularly charged with beliefs, fears and hopes surrounding the future of those who are sick. The third chapter, therefore, addresses four of the classic issues surrounding each sacrament: matter and form, the minister, the subject, and the sacramental effects. These four elements of sacramental liturgy link the current rite of anointing to its earlier articulation as extreme unction and forward to future issues within the Church.

Beyond the intra-ecclesial concerns of the elements of the rite, however, is the way that the sacrament of the anointing of the sick and its broader context of all pastoral care of the sick exemplify the Church in the world. The experience of sickness, the continuing evolution of the rites of healing, the interpretation of Scripture, the role of the Church, the relationship between the Church and the medical arts, corporate understandings of the human person, and of the role of family and friends, all raise questions that have, in turn, influenced the theological and ecclesial context in which these rites unfold. These final questions will be grouped into four areas: what is the relationship between the Church's care for the sick and the world of professional medical care; what is the relationship between the Church's care for the sick and the cultural context of much of the experience of being sick in the United States today; what is the meaning of suffering in light of these issues; and what is the relationship between the anointing of the sick and the care for the dying in the lived reality of the twenty-first century.

The PCS has offered to the Church a wealth of assistance in visiting the sick, in praying with the sick, in facilitating services of communion, and in tailoring the sacramental rites of anointing and viaticum to meet the particular circumstances of each individual illness and journey into death. The focus of this study is on the heart of the whole spectrum of pastoral care of the sick, namely the sacrament of the anointing of the sick, and the reader is encouraged to consult the entire rite, to pray the prayers, to read the recommended scriptural texts, and to imagine the various environments for which each of the optional structures was designed. Throughout the following chapters there are extensive excerpts from the PCS, but keeping the official rite close at hand will result in a more fruitful reading of the various issues.

Notes, Introduction

[1] Decree of the Sacred Congregation for Divine Worship, 7 December 1972.

[2] Bishop John Cummins (Chairman, BCL), *Foreword to the American Version of Pastoral Care of the Sick* (Collegeville: Pueblo, 1990) 776.

[3] In addition to the official rite, Pastoral Care of the Sick, the Book of Blessings, promulgated in 1989, contains more prayers, Scripture passages, and blessings in several ritual patterns, often made use of pastorally through the *Shorter Book of Blessings* (New York: Catholic Book Publishing Co., 1990) 140–80.

[4] Mary Collins, "The Roman Ritual: Pastoral Care and Anointing of the Sick," *Concilium* 1991/2, ed. Mary Collins and David N. Power (London: SCM Press, 1991) 4.

[5] The issue of who may be the recipient of the anointing of the sick has engendered a recurring discussion since the rite was first promulgated in 1972 (and in the years preceding that with its preparations). The issue will be further discussed in chs. 1 and 2 of this work.

[6] "Of or pertaining to a pastor or shepherd of souls; having relation to the spiritual care or guidance of a 'flock' or body of Christians" (*The Oxford English Dictionary*, Vol. XI, ed. J. A. Simpson and E.S.C. Weiner [Oxford: Clarendon Press, 1989] 324).

[7] Elaine Ramshaw, *Ritual and Pastoral Care* (Philadelphia: Fortress Press, 1987) 16.

[8] See particularly paragraph 5 of the "General Introduction," which draws on the model of Christ for ritual as an expression of care: "The Lord himself showed great concern for the bodily and spiritual welfare of the sick and commanded his followers to do likewise."

[9] Revised edition 1989, New York: Pueblo Publishing Co.

[10] PCS 43.

[11] Gusmer, *And You Visited Me*, 53.

[12] "Music in Catholic Worship" was the fruit of the 1968 publication of the BCL *(Musicam Sacram)* further adapted and critiqued by the FDLC, which published MCW in 1972.

[13] MCW 41.

[14] Based on the pastoral practice of anointing at dying, the scholastic theological development focused on "extreme unction as a preparation for the passage from this life to the next, and discussed its effect as a preparation for glory . . . ." Trent's teaching on the sacrament, which in the preliminary text asserted that the sacrament was to be administered "only to those who are in their final struggle and have come to grips with death and are about to go forth to the Lord," was altered in the final text to read that "this anointing is to be used for the sick, but especially for those who are so dangerously ill as to appear at the point of departing this life" (Michael G. Lawler, *Symbol and Sacrament: A Contemporary Sacramental Theology* [Omaha, NE: Creighton University Press, 1995] 165).

[15] Vatican Council II, "Constitution on the Liturgy," art. 73, AAS 56 (1964) 118–19.

[16] My own work with the NACC (National Association of Catholic Chaplains) in 1995 in drawing up a white paper on anointing of the sick resulted in an interesting survey on the availability of ordained priests, particularly in hospital/hospice situations. See The National Association of Catholic Chaplains, *Survey on the Sacrament of the Anointing of the Sick* (Edwin Fonner, Jr., Dr Ph, 1995).

[17] In addition to being the theological premise for this whole book series on the sacraments, *lex orandi, lex credendi* is a reduction of a complex and disputed historical tag calling attention to the need for an alignment between what we believe and what we pray. A good overview of the difficulties in interpreting the original phrase of Prosper of Aquitaine can be found in Maxwell Johnson, "Liturgy and Theology," *Liturgy in Dialogue: Essays in Memory of Ronald Jasper* (Collegeville: Liturgical Press, 1993) 203–27.

Chapter One

An Overview of the Rites of Pastoral Care of the Sick

Theological understandings drawn from liturgical texts and from the enactment of actual liturgical rites based on those texts presume a close reading of both the texts themselves, scriptural and liturgical, as well as the structure of the overall rite. In other words, studying the written version of a liturgy as well as the actual doing of that liturgy implies engaging with the texts and how the texts are juxtaposed one with another and with all the elements that make up the "orchestration of the rite,"[1] including actions, physical objects, music, environment, and, above all, the individual and communal gathering of the participants. The same text can evoke a very different response or interpretation in one liturgical structure as opposed to another, often because the juxtaposition of the liturgical event with the text is so different that the perception of the text, or texts, or actions changes because of the context. In spite of this, the academic fields of liturgical history and liturgical theology have in the past relied almost solely on the study of written words, to the detriment of understanding how the very arrangement of the pieces of the liturgy contribute to our understanding of meaning.[2] In the remainder of this chapter, we will broaden that view of a particular set of liturgical rites in looking at the structure of the rituals for the sick, first by stepping back and viewing the whole collection of rites and then by moving in and focusing on the heart of the rite, namely the sacrament of the anointing of the sick. Finally, because the whole collection of rituals that make up the Pastoral Care of the Sick so clearly find their literal source in the actions and directives of Christ as revealed in Scripture, in addition to being fundamentally patterned in a biblical way,[3] we will conclude by reviewing some scholarship on the two key biblical passages, Mark 6:13 and James 5:13-15.

The Structure of the Rites for the Sick

The structure of *Pastoral Care of the Sick: Rites of Anointing and Viaticum* (hereafter PCS) is divided into three main parts. Part I, "Pastoral Care of the Sick," contains three chapters on visiting the sick (one for adults, one for children, and one for visits which include communion of the sick in various circumstances), and an extended chapter on anointing of the sick that contains various combinations of texts and rituals for differing circumstances. Part II, "Pastoral Care of the Dying," is composed of an extended chapter on the celebration of viaticum with options for different situations, a chapter on the commendation of the dying, a chapter on prayers for the dead, and a chapter on rites for exceptional circumstances, which include continuous rites of penance and anointing, rites for emergencies, and Christian initiation for the dying. Part III contains the scriptural resources for all of the rites mentioned above and an appendix with the rite of reconciliation of individual penitents adapted to the circumstances of the sick.

A brief glance at the outline reviewed above is revelatory with regard to the theology emerging from the structure of these rites, particularly in two areas. First, it is amazingly extensive and rich, both in its scope of resources and in its flexibility for the many circumstances in which the sick and those who minister with them find themselves. The structure of the rites as a whole indicates the centrality of context that nuances the theology of anointing and pastoral care of the sick in general. These are not abstract, generic rituals, but rituals shaped by particular circumstances. Different circumstances call for different rituals, and the corresponding discernment required of the minister is far greater than that of more fixed rites. Second, for a rite titled "Pastoral Care of the Sick," it may seem odd that half of the content and intent is actually for the dying and the dead. While the reality of interpreting what "seriously" sick means is quite broad, the pastoral practicality of this combination of rites together is clear. The balance in the overall structure of the whole rite may give pause to those of us who argue too strongly for a discontinuity between the pre-conciliar and post-conciliar rites of anointing the sick, particularly with regard to the pre-conciliar concern on the seriousness of the illness. Context is text,[4] and here the context of the rite itself links the pastoral care of the sick with all of its rich meanings to the rites for the dying and dead and the rites of penance throughout all of the options. How are both of these issues, flexibility and juxtaposition, to be interpreted through the lens of liturgical theology? A more detailed analysis of the pivotal rite of anointing of the sick will establish the foundation for later chapters to propose some understandings of these questions. What follows is an overview of the anointing of the sick with blessed oil and the accompanying words and gestures, as they literally stand at the center of the arrangement of these rites and at the heart of the sacrament of the sick.

Anointing of the Sick

Anointing Outside Mass

Introductory Rites (115–118)
    Greeting (115)
    Sprinkling with Holy Water (116)
    Instruction (117)
    Penitential Rite (118)
Liturgy of the Word (119–120)
    Reading (119)
    Response (120)
Liturgy of Anointing (121–126)
    Litany (121)
    Laying on of Hands (122)
    Prayer over the Oil (123)
    Anointing (124)
    Prayer after Anointing (125)
    The Lord's Prayer (126)
Liturgy of Holy Communion (127–129)
    Communion (127)
    Silent Prayer (128)
    Prayer after Communion (129)
Concluding Rite (130)
    Blessing (130)

The first set of ritual texts in Chapter IV of PCS is titled "Anointing Outside Mass," implying by its primary position that this is the normative structure of the rite. After a theological and practical introduction of fourteen paragraphs (97–110)[5] plus four brief paragraphs pertaining to the specifics of anointing outside of Eucharist, the rite is presented in fivefold shape (Introductory Rites, Liturgy of the Word, Liturgy of Anointing, Liturgy of Holy Communion, and Concluding Rite).

The Introductory Rites include the greeting (115), optional sprinkling with holy water (116), instruction, based on the James "urtext" of anointing (117), and penitential rite in three optional forms (118). Because the focus of the instruction based on James at 117 is so crucial to the whole rite, it is reproduced here:

> My dear friends, we are gathered here in the name of our Lord Jesus Christ who is present among us. As the gospels relate, the sick came to him for healing; moreover, he loves us so much that he died for our sake. Through the apostle James, he has commanded us: "Are there any who are sick among you? Let them send for the priests of the Church, and let the priests pray over them, anointing them with oil in the name of the Lord; and the prayer of faith will save the sick persons, and the Lord will raise them up; and if they have committed any sins, their sins will be forgiven them." Let us therefore commend our sick brother/sister N. to the grace and power of Christ, that he may save him/her and raise him/her up.

The Liturgy of the Word includes three suggested readings (119) with more possibilities drawn from Part III (the expanded collection of scriptural and liturgical texts), and an optional "response" (homily, 120).

The Liturgy of Anointing is composed of a litany of optional length (121), the laying on of hands in silence (122), prayer over the oil (123), which is either a thanksgiving over oil already blessed or an actual blessing of oil (with some optional forms of the blessing found at 140 and 248), the anointing itself (124), the prayer after anointing (125) with a number of prayer options specific to person and situation, and the Lord's Prayer (126).

The Liturgy of Holy Communion follows with the showing of the eucharistic bread to those present (127) and a reference back to no. 88 that is the invitation to communion and the distribution of communion. Communion concludes with silent prayer (128) and three options for prayer after communion (129), which vary appropriately for different circumstances. The concluding rite is simply a blessing (130) with four possible texts and an optional rubric to bless (in silence) with the Blessed Sacrament if any remains.

The heart of the rite, as presented in the General Introduction (5), is the laying on of hands, the offering of the prayer of faith, and the anointing.[6] These outward ritual actions and words effect the sacrament:

> This sacrament gives the grace of the Holy Spirit to those who are sick: by this grace the whole person is helped and saved, sustained by trust in God, and strengthened against the temptations of the Evil One and against anxiety over death. Thus the sick person is able not only to bear suffering bravely, but also to fight against it. A return to physical health may follow the reception of this sacrament if it will be beneficial to the sick person's salvation. If necessary, the sacrament also provides the sick person with the forgiveness of sins and the completion of Christian penance. (6)

Anointing Within Mass

Introductory Rites (135–136)
  Reception of the Sick (135)
  Opening Prayer (136)
Liturgy of the Word (137)
Liturgy of Anointing (138–146)
  Litany (138)
  Laying on of Hands (139)
  Prayer over the Oil (140)
  Anointing (141)
  Prayer after Anointing (142)
Liturgy of the Eucharist (143)
  Prayer over the Gifts (144)
  Eucharistic Prayer (145)
  Prayer after Communion (146)
Concluding Rites (147–148)
  Dismissal (148)

The second ritual section is "Anointing Within Mass," for which the opening paragraph of the Introduction offers an explanation of the particular circumstances in which this secondary context might be appropriate: "When the condition of the sick person permits, and especially when communion is to be received, the sacrament of anointing may be celebrated within Mass" (131). The second introductory paragraph describes the normative rationale for this liturgy: "This rite may be used to anoint a number of people within the same celebration. It is especially appropriate for large gatherings of a diocese, parish, or society for the sick, or for pilgrimages."[7] This adapted rite for anointing, therefore, is dependent on the ability of the sick person to participate in a longer and more complex liturgy as well as to make allowances for corporate celebrations in which large numbers of people may be receiving the sacrament. As with the "Anointing Outside Mass" preference is given to celebrating the sacrament of penance at a convenient time before the liturgy (113, 133).[8] The rite is presented in the same fivefold shape as "Anointing Outside Mass," but with the "Liturgy of Holy Communion" replaced here with the "Liturgy of the Eucharist."

The Introductory Rites are structured in a far simpler manner, beginning with the Greeting, which is not immediately discernible in the edited arrangement of the study text.[9] The Greeting, once found, is followed by the Reception of the Sick with two optional texts (135), which paragraph 109 describes as "a sympathetic expression of Christ's concern for those who are ill and of the role of the sick in the people of God."

> We have come together to celebrate the sacraments of anointing and eucharist. Christ is always present when we gather in his name; today we welcome him especially as physician and healer. We pray that the sick may be restored to health by the gift of his mercy and made whole in his fullness. (135A)

> Christ taught his disciples to be a community of love. In praying together, in sharing all things, and in caring for the sick, they recalled his words: "Insofar as you did this to one of these, you did it to me." We gather today to witness to this teaching and to pray in the name of Jesus the healer that the sick may be restored to health. Through this eucharist and anointing we invoke his healing power. (135B)

The Reception, which functions as a catechetical introduction to the rite, is followed by the opening prayer (136) presented with two options. The Liturgy of the Word "is celebrated in the usual way according to the instructions in no. 134" (137) which points the reader to The Lectionary for Mass, or Part III of PCS, inclusive of the homily but exclusive of the general intercessions. The Liturgy of Anointing follows the same ritual shape as "Anointing Outside Mass" but has some textual differences as well as necessary adaptations for moving prayers from the singular to the plural. The Litany (138) has the same thematic as number 121 but in a different order, with more attention to all who care for the sick. Both litanies conclude with the petition that leads to the laying on of hands: "Give life and health to our brothers and sisters on whom we lay our hands in your name"(138). The Laying on of Hands (139) is adapted for several priests: "each one lays hands on some of the sick." The Prayer Over the Oil (140) contains the same text for Thanksgiving over Blessed Oil but adds another blessing prayer for oil that follows the Thanksgiving prayer exactly until the last petition. Unlike the first option presented at paragraph 123, it does not contain the classic pneumatological language of epiclesis. In addition, the "Anointing Within Mass" does not refer the reader to the "emergency" text of number 248 (under "Continuous Rite of Penance, Anointing, and Viaticum"). The Anointing (141) and the Prayer after Anointing (142) follow the earlier outline with adaptations for large numbers of sick people and additional priests, except that the options for "Before Surgery," "For a Child," and "For a Young Person," are not offered. The Liturgy of the Eucharist continues with two proper Prayers over the Gifts (144) and optional embolisms for Eucharistic Prayers I, II, and III. The rite presumes a normative eucharistic celebration apart from these texts as no. 146 jumps to the proper "Prayer After Communion" (two options). The Concluding Rites (147) contain the same blessing options but in a different order. The interesting note for the Dismissal (148) instructs the deacon to dismiss the people and commend "the sick to their care" without, however, a sample text. Under the earlier instructions for "Anointing of the Sick with a Large Congregation," number 109 says that this "celebration may conclude with an appropriate song."

Anointing in a Hospital or Institution

> Introductory Rites (154–155)
>> Greeting (154)
>> Instruction (155)
> Liturgy of Anointing (156–159)
>> Laying on of Hands (156)
>> Anointing (157)
>> The Lord's Prayer (158)
>> Prayer after Anointing (159)
> Concluding Rite (160)
>> Blessing (160)

The third section in Chapter IV on Anointing of the Sick is a brief explanation of the necessary adaptations in more intimate rituals (and often those under greater time pressures and physical limitations) that take place in hospitals, nursing homes, or other institutions. Fundamentally, the adaptations are abbreviations, as the first of five introductory paragraphs explains: "The rite which follows is a simplification of the anointing rite and preserves its central elements. It is intended for those occasions when only the priest and sick person are present and the complete rite cannot be celebrated" (149). The introductory paragraphs remind the presider to inquire about the "physical and spiritual condition of the sick person in order to plan the celebration properly and choose the appropriate prayers" (150), as well as to "arrange for the continued pastoral care of the sick person, especially for frequent opportunities to receive communion" (153). Paragraph 152 reiterates the preference for the fullness of the rite by suggesting that because of the circumstances in medical emergency facilities it may be desirable to postpone the sacrament if possible.[10] While liturgically this makes absolute sense because the fullness of the rite is always more desirable, pastorally it is often *only* in these emergency situations that calling the chaplain or priest comes to the collective mind of the family members or friends gathered around a critically injured or ill person.

The Introductory Rites consist of a Greeting (154, two options are printed, the first and the last options of number 81 in Communion to the Sick) and the Instruction, which refers back to number 117, the teaching based on the James text, but offers a version of the instruction now in the form of an opening prayer:

> Lord God, / you have said to us through your apostle James: / "Are there people sick among you? / Let them send for the priests of the Church, / and let the priests pray over them / anointing them with oil in the name of the Lord. / The prayer of faith will save the sick persons, / and the Lord will raise them up. / If they have committed any sins, / their sins will be forgiven them."

> Lord, / we have gathered here in your name / and we ask you to be among us, / to watch over our brother/sister N. / We ask this with confidence, / for you live and reign for ever and ever. Amen. (155)

While the prayer text is a bit wordy with the same teaching text underlying it, it combines the instruction and most of the preparatory elements spread throughout the other anointing rites under Introductory Rites and Liturgy of the Word. A rubric allowing for the sacrament of penance to be celebrated is included after this opening prayer, granted that this is a one-on-one celebration of the anointing.[11]

The Liturgy of Anointing begins immediately with the Laying on of Hands (156) and the Anointing (157 with reference back to 124). The Lord's Prayer and the Prayer after Anointing are in the reverse order of Anointing Outside Mass, the Lord's Prayer coming first (158) and then the Prayer after Anointing (159), which refers the reader back to 125, with its seven options for varying circumstances.

The rite ends simply with a Blessing (160 with two options, B and D from Anointing Outside Mass) in the Concluding Rite. The heart of the rite remains in this abbreviated version, consistent with the teaching of the General Introduction to the Anointing of the Sick that focuses on the Prayer of Faith, the Laying on of Hands and the Anointing with Oil.

Scriptural Foundation of the Anointing of the Sick

> They cast out many demons, and anointed with oil many who were sick and cured them. (Mark 6:13)
>
> Are there any among you suffering? They should pray. Are any cheerful? They should sing songs of praise. Are any among you sick? They should call for the elders of the church and have them pray over them, anointing them with oil in the name of the Lord. The prayer of faith will save the sick, and the Lord will raise them up; and anyone who has committed sins will be forgiven." (Jas 5:13-15)[12]

In both the Decree establishing the new sacramental form (1972) and the Apostolic Constitution promulgating the new rite (1972), the scriptural warrant is prominent in the opening paragraphs. The Decree bases the Church's ministry on the actions of Jesus himself, referring to Mark 16:18, and the Constitution establishes the scriptural foundation of the sacrament with reference to Mark 6:13 but relying most particularly on James 5:14-15, which is quoted in full at the beginning of the text of Paul VI. The General Introduction to the Anointing of the Sick refers to Mark 6:13 when expressing that the anointing is done in the "name and with the power of Christ himself" (98), and acknowledges that throughout the New Testament healing is an omnipresent activity of Jesus and of the disciples, revealing the present reign of God and functioning as a sign of wholeness and salvation promised through the

Christ. A much-quoted summary of this is found in Matthew's Gospel: "Then Jesus went about all the cities and villages, teaching in their synagogues, and proclaiming the good news of the kingdom, and curing every disease and every sickness" (Matt 9:35).

The single verse in question in Mark falls within the first half of that Gospel, generally understood as describing "Jesus' activity in Galilee and beyond (1:16–8:21)."[13] Within the overall theology of Mark, where disciples and other followers rarely understand the true meaning of Jesus' life and ministry, Mark 6:13 comes in the more "positive stories in the Gospel," falling within a section "relating the call of the first disciples"[14] and the descriptions of the heart of their mission. The verse is contextualized by a sense of urgency in mission in verses 8-11, which reaches the climax in verses 12 and 13. There the proclamation of the good news is found in the preaching that leads to repentance, the casting out of demons, and the anointing with oil to heal. The anointing with oil *(aléipho)* is the same word used in James 5:14, not an anointing as a first sign of honor or recognition, but rather a literal pouring of oil on the recipient as with ointment. This particular word is only found eight times in the New Testament in a variety of anointing stories. The conclusion of Robert Leaney, one of the few authors to focus specifically on Mark 6:13, was that the evidence within the context of Mark points

> to the conclusion that the ministry of healing derives from that of reconciliation, that the Lord in his Galilean ministry did not charge the disciples with a task of physical healing primarily, but that when they went out, 'they proclaimed that men should repent, and they cast out many demons, and they anointed many sick with oil, and healed.' Thus might Mark remind us of our duty to unite what ought never to have been divided, the ministry to spirit, mind and body.[15]

His conclusions, as well as biblical scholars situating the verse within its Markan context, point to a healing of the psychosomatic whole as focus, much like that of the James text on which the current rite is structurally dependent.

The instruction of number 117 in the rite (and its prayer form in number 155) both point to the dependence of the rite on James. This use of an instruction at the beginning of a rite (rather than an introduction or instruction folded into the homily) is a rare form for a contemporary sacramental rite, reflecting the concern of those responsible for its promulgation that the rite be seen in a new light rather than simply as a translation of the pre-conciliar extreme unction.

Many fine exegetical and theological commentaries have been produced on the section of the Letter of James in question[16] and have dealt with the controversial issues around the translation of particular words or phrases.[17] While the translation issues are important in understanding the context of the James passage and how it was heard in the early Church, it is clear that the contemporary rite has been faithful to the primary ritual shape of the biblical passage. The James text moves from the situational question in verse 14 ("Are any among you sick?") to the three actions proposed: 1) "They should call for the elders of the church"; 2) "have them pray over them"; 3) "anoint them with oil." The text then moves to the two primary effects described in verse 14: 1) "The prayer of faith will save the sick," and "the Lord will raise them up"; 2) "and anyone who has committed sins will be forgiven." The rite of anointing the sick follows this theologically and ritually by reminding the Church that, "in public and private catechesis, the faithful should be educated to ask for the sacrament of anointing . . . they should not follow the wrongful practice of delaying the reception of the sacrament" (13).

And yet there are some differences in emphasis here between the foundational verses in James and its contemporary expression. The James text, in asking if any are sick *(asthenei),* uses a noun that does not limit the illness to the category of serious or grave illness but is more general in application.[18] The General Introduction for PCS, in the section titled "Recipients of the Anointing of the Sick," focuses on the anointing being for those who are "seriously impaired" (8), with its extensive and well-known footnote describing the difficulty of translating the Latin *periculose.*[19] A great deal of the official introductory material in both introductions and in most of the secondary literature focuses on this issue: how sick is sick enough to receive the sacrament of anointing? The difficulty underlying the extensive writing on the subject is a desire to balance encouraging the faithful to request the sacrament in good time ("The priest should ensure . . . that the celebration takes place while the sick person is capable of active participation" [99]), in other words, not to wait until the moment of death, but at the same time not to treat the sacrament lightly, using it for minor illnesses that are not impacting the whole person or that involve only physical illness.

The latter issue calls attention to another point of distinction between James and the contemporary rite in defining "sick," a distinction based in translation as well as cultural and historical differences in the perception of the human being. Charles Gusmer points out that James "is unaware of the distinction between sin and sickness as we know it," so that for him "the subject of the anointing is a complete sick person, a psychosomatic unity, and the expected result is a restoration of the whole person."[20] The cultural and linguistic differences regarding how much of the human person is being addressed has complicated the multiple effects of the threefold ritual actions, historically isolating spiritual healing from physical healing. Our postmodern view of the human being is gradually recapturing some of that sense of "psychosomatic unity" but we still tend to isolate the physical, emotional, and mental dimensions (and most noticeably the spiritual dimension) in the scientific and the ritual realms, to the extent that we must ultimately address them separately in spite of our knowledge of the interconnected realities.

The three actions laid out in the James text—calling the elders of the Church, having them pray over the sick person, and anointing the sick with oil—form the heart of the contemporary rite. The sick person is a member of a community who calls upon the community to assist in times of sickness, and the community is represented or embodied in the official leaders, the *presbyteroi* (as opposed to the potentially individual, charismatic healers described in 1 Corinthians 12).[21] The historical development of the anointing of the sick witnesses to the need for the person to truly be a member of the Christian community, and the General Introduction reiterates that by reminding the minister of anointing that the sacrament is "not to be conferred on anyone who remains obdurately in open and serious sin"(15),[22] in other words, someone who has removed themselves from the communion of the Church. The controversial translation of *presbyteroi* as "priests"[23] is consistent with the current restrictions on the minister of the rite, most clearly laid out in nos. 16–19 of the General Instruction ("The priest is the only proper minister of the anointing of the sick" 16).[24]

The actions of the *presbyteroi,* once summoned, are twofold. They pray over the sick person, implying a physical closeness ("pray *over,* not *for*"[25]) between the official representatives of the Church and the sick individual. The liturgy of anointing in the rites begins with a Litany of Prayer that leads into and continues in the Laying on of Hands, an early Church adaptation of the scriptural mandate to "pray over."[26] The anointing with oil *(auton elaío)* uses the more generic verb for anointing, *aléipho,* "anoint" or "pour oil over" in probable continuity with widespread cultural uses of oil for sickness. Very early in Church history the oil is understood as efficacious because of its having been set apart for this ritual, either blessed by a bishop or blessed by a martyr (the oil was run through the tomb), both of which expressed the ecclesial dimension of divine presence and made private or domestic anointing acts of the Church. The current rite retains this post-scriptural practice by including a prayer of thanksgiving over oil already blessed or, if necessary, blessing the oil at this point in the rite. The General Instruction is clear about the preference given to oil blessed by the bishop, preferably at the Chrism Mass of Holy Thursday (21), with the exceptions noted in number 21b and in number 22.[27]

The anointing itself, done in the "name of the Lord," is not elaborated in the James text, aside from the clarity about doing it in the Lord's name, which seems to distinguish the action from the everyday anointings that were necessary in a hot, dry climate and for those done for the soothing of skin and the healing of infirmities.[28] It calls to mind the text of Mark 6:13 which may have influenced the James verse[29] and contextualizes the whole prayer-anointing sequence. The contemporary rite of anointing reflects a considerable abbreviation and simplification of centuries of increasing complexity in the method of anointing since New Testament times, and is accompanied by a formula that is ambiguously trinitarian. Because "the Lord" is not clearly defined in the James text, the lack of clarity about "the Lord" in the current formula is probably in greater continuity with the scriptural warrant than intervening centuries. Of the seven prayer options that follow the anointing, two are addressed to the Second Person of the Trinity and echo the "name of the Lord" most clearly[30] as it is popularly understood among Christians.

> Lord Jesus Christ, our Redeemer, / by the grace of your Holy Spirit / cure the weakness of your servant N. / Heal his/her sickness and forgive his/her sins; / expel all afflictions of mind and body; / mercifully restore him/her to full health, / and enable him/her to resume his/her former duties, / for you are Lord for ever and ever. Amen. (125B)

> Lord Jesus Christ, / you chose to share our human nature, / to redeem all people, and to heal the sick.

> Look with compassion upon your servant N., / whom we have anointed in your name with this holy oil / for the healing of his/her body and spirit. / Support him/her with your power, / comfort him/her with your protection, / and give him/her the strength to fight against evil.

> Since you have given him/her a share in your own passion, / help him/her to find hope in suffering, for you are Lord for ever and ever. Amen. (125C)

As mentioned above, the James text does not indicate how or on what parts of the body the anointing was done, and the number and placement of anointings has varied greatly throughout the Christian history of anointing.[31] In the contemporary rite, the ritual application of the anointing, customarily on the forehead and hands, is accompanied by the bipartite formula summarizing images from James. "Through this holy anointing may the Lord in his love and mercy help you with the grace of the Holy Spirit" is pronounced as the forehead is anointed, "May the Lord who frees you from sin save you and raise you up" accompanies the anointing of hands (124). The latter phrase is clearly drawn from the "results" or desired effects of verse 14 in the James text, recalling the holistic healing of body and soul and the relationship between sin and sickness, not as causal or inevitable but as a possible part of the overall illness ("If he has committed any sins . . ."). This indirect relation between the anointing and forgiveness of sins in James receives a slightly different but also indirect verbal treatment in the contemporary formula.

The language of physical healing in James reiterates the holistic view of sickness and health described above: "the prayer of faith will save *(sosei)* the sick," a verb used by James elsewhere to describe the "salvation of one's soul" (Jas 1:21; 2:14; 4:12; 5:20) as well as common in gospel passages with a "double meaning—either eternal salvation or restoration to health."[32] The use of the word *egerein* ("to raise up") also has a double meaning in New Testament use, either to be raised up as in resurrection ("raising from the dead" such as in 1 Cor 15:15, 29, 32, 35, 42-44; 2 Cor 1:9; 4:14) or to be "lifted up" from sickness, "raising to life and health" (Matt 9:5-7; Mark 1:31; 2:9; 5:41; 9:27).[33] The direct borrowing of these words in translation in the contemporary rite seems to imply again a theological understanding of holistic healing of body and soul, physical healing and the forgiveness of sins.

In addition to these examples of the relationship between the scriptural texts as source and the contemporary rite, the biblical pattern of liturgy is also evident in the rite. In speaking of the life-giving juxtaposition of "an old book and this present people,"[34] Gordon Lathrop says that

> the old stories and our condition of need, loss, and death do indeed correspond. Hearing the Bible, we are gathered into a story, we have a place for our sorrow to sink. At the same time, the liturgical vision is that these stories mediate to us an utterly new thing, beyond all texts. Juxtaposed to this assembly, the texts are understood by the liturgy to have been transformed to speak now the presence of God's

grace. In this way, the texts are made to carry us, who have heard the text and been included in its evocations into this very transformation: God's grace is present in our lives. Texts are read here as if they were the concrete medium for the encounter with God.[35]

Beyond the Markan and Jacobite texts which give dominical authority to the rite of anointing the sick, the Scripture selections chosen for the celebration of the sacrament provide varied avenues for the "encounter with God" that every liturgy is about. Looking at just the first of three suggested gospel texts in the "Anointing Outside Mass" will suffice to exemplify both the care that must be taken in wisely using the flexibility of the rite, as well as the biblical pattern of the liturgy through God's initiative in speaking, our response and our transformation in and through the word to the new Word spoken in the actual ritual event.

The first suggested reading for the anointing of the sick is Matthew 11:25-30:

> At that time Jesus said, "I thank you, Father, Lord of heaven and earth, because you have hidden these things from the wise and the intelligent and have revealed them to infants; yes, Father, for such was your gracious will. All things have been handed over to me by my Father; and no one knows the Son except the Father, and no one knows the Father except the Son and anyone to whom the Son chooses to reveal him. Come to me, all you that are weary and are carrying heavy burdens, and I will give you rest. Take my yoke upon you, and learn from me; for I am gentle and humble in heart, and you will find rest for your souls. For my yoke is easy, and my burden is light."

All

The second is Mark 2:1-12:

> When Jesus returned to Capernaum after some days, it was reported that he was at home. So many gathered around that there was no longer room for them, not even in front of the door, and he was speaking the word to them. Then some people came, bringing to him a paralyzed man, carried by four of them. And when they could not bring him to Jesus because of the crowd, they removed the roof above him, and after having dug through it, they let down the mat on which the paralytic lay. When Jesus saw their faith, he said to the paralytic, "Son, your sins are forgiven." Now some of the scribes were sitting there, questioning in their hearts, "Why does this fellow speak in this way? It is blasphemy! Who can forgive sins but God alone?" At once Jesus perceived in his spirit that they were discussing these questions among themselves, and he said to them, "Why do you raise such questions in your hearts?

> Which is easier, to say to the paralytic, 'Your sins are forgiven,' or to say, 'Stand up and take your mat and walk'? But so that you may know that the Son of Man has authority on earth to forgive sins"—he said to the paralytic—"I say to you, stand up, take your mat and go to your home." And he stood up, and immediately took the mat and went out before all of them, so that they were all amazed and glorified God, saying, "We have never seen anything like this!"

The third reading is Luke 7:18b-23:

> So John summoned two of his disciples and sent them to the Lord to ask, "Are you the one who is to come, or are we to wait for another?" When the men had come to him, they said, "John the Baptist has sent us to you to ask, 'Are you the one who is to come, or are we to wait for another?'" Jesus had just then cured many people of diseases, plagues, and evil spirits, and had given sight to many who were blind. And he answered them, "Go and tell John what you have seen and heard: the blind receive their sight, the lame walk, the lepers are cleansed, the deaf hear, the dead are raised, the poor have good news brought to them. And blessed is anyone who takes no offense at me."

While there are many more suggested readings in the scriptural appendix of Part III of the larger rite, these three gospel selections are incorporated into the actual rite of anointing the sick itself, and therefore take some priority in use. But the variety of images in just these three texts is quite rich. Using the first text from Matthew, one interpretation that could be heard in the midst of the anointing of the sick is the promise of the comforting presence of Jesus, who calls the one carrying a heavy burden of illness and suggests that the burden is that of Jesus himself. The Scripture text gathers us in, "We have a place for our sorrow to sink."[36] This narrative theology of sacramental encounter effects, by the contextualizing of the text, one of the key points of the *praenotanda*, namely that Christianity does not promise that there will be no suffering, but that suffering and sickness, when they come, will have meaning:

> Christians feel and experience pain as do all other people; yet their faith helps them to grasp more deeply the mystery of suffering and to bear their pain with greater courage. From Christ's words they know that sickness has meaning and value for their own salvation and for the salvation of the world. (1)

The juxtaposition of this Word of God with the litany of prayer immediately follows; the laying on of hands and the anointing with oil speak of the "presence of God's grace" with different voices. As with all liturgical gatherings, "the intention of the liturgy is to manifest the presence of God in this assembly, a merciful presence that is meant not just for this assembly but for the world."[37] Here particularly the uniting of the suffering of the individual Christian is joined to that of Christ's, which, in itself, becomes a witness to Christ, and through Christ to the Father. This witness is not just for "this assembly" but also for the whole world ("From Christ's words they know that sickness has meaning and value for their own salvation and for the salvation of the world"). So the context of the rite of the anointing of the sick, the context of the situation of the individual who is sick, the context of the ritual actions of laying on of hands, of anointing, and of communion, all of these interpret the Scripture proclaimed, allowing it to emphasize different aspects of the biblical pattern of liturgy, which becomes a pattern for Christian living. The other two gospel readings from Mark and Luke may draw out other aspects of the rite: Mark, in particular, juxtaposed with the James text and the anointing formula emphasizing the forgiveness of sins as spiritual healing and physical healing, and Luke emphasizing the healing as sign of the reign of God already begun in the midst of the assembly, in the midst of the world, and in the pilgrimage of the individual Christian towards union with God.

The scriptural basis of the revised rite of anointing of the sick is apparent, both in its use of Scripture as defining theology and ritual structure, and in the biblical pattern of liturgy and life that flows from the juxtapositions. This faithfulness to the normative character of Scripture is striking in both the close adherence in text and ritual structure of the contemporary rite to the James text, as well as highlighting the interesting dichotomy between a wealth of theological interpretations available in Scripture and the dearth of ritual examples on which to base contemporary rites. But, as with all the sacramental rites, the normative theological and ritual foundation of the New Testament is augmented and interpreted by historical and theological development, cultural understandings, and doctrinal systemization. With those expansions in mind, we turn to a more detailed investigation of the three primary ritual components of the anointing of the sick: the prayer of faith, which is the overarching context for all the actions of the rite, the laying on of hands, and the anointing of the sick.

Notes, Chapter One

[1] Robert S. Ellwood, *Introducing Religion from Inside and Outside*, 3rd ed. (Englewood Cliffs, NJ: Prentice Hall, 1993) 83.

[2] See Gordon W. Lathrop, *Holy Things: A Liturgical Theology* (Minneapolis: Fortress Press, 1993), for a contemporary overview of the theological meaning imparted not just by the words but also by the arrangement of texts, actions, things and people in the liturgy.

[3] "Whatever the assembly means, it means by juxtaposing an old book and this present people" (ibid., 16). The biblical pattern of God's initiative and human response as re-enacted again and again in liturgy through listening and responding, as well as the dialogical nature of all liturgy, is not just at the basis of eucharistic liturgy, but also the other sacramental rites as well, including the anointing of the sick.

[4] See Kevin W. Irwin, *Context and Text: Method in Liturgical Theology* (Collegeville: Liturgical Press, 1994) especially Part 2.

[5] The numbering of the paragraphs for *Pastoral Care of the Sick: Rites of Anointing and Viaticum* is that of the Bishops' Committee on the Liturgy (National Conference of Catholic Bishops). The paragraph numbers deviate from the original Latin due to the pastoral rearrangement of the document in its current English language and American adapted version. "In undertaking the pastoral rearrangement of *Ordo Unctionis Infirmorum eorumque pastoralis curae* it was necessary to depart from the numbering system employed in the Latin edition. The General Introduction corresponds exactly to the Latin introduction. Beginning with number 42, however, the present numbering system diverges from the Latin system" (John S. Cummins, Bishop of Oakland, in the Foreword). This study uses the most recent edition published through the Liturgical Press, Volume One of *The Rites of the Catholic Church*, 1990.

[6] "The celebration of this sacrament consists especially in the laying on of hands by the priests of the church, the offering of the prayer of faith, and the anointing of the sick with oil made holy by God's blessing. This rite signifies the grace of the sacrament and confers it" (PCS 5).

[7] The paragraph directs the reader to nos. 108–10, "Anointing of the Sick with a Large Congregation," which includes directions for multiple anointings and singular prayers as well as directions for diocesan bishops to assure that only those "whose health is seriously impaired by sickness or old age" participate in the anointing (108).

[8] There are four paragraphs of introduction total in this section, with the final paragraph (134) focusing on vestments, proper readings, and proscribed days for this Mass.

[9] The presider must refer back to no. 109, which refers back to no. 135, but actually can find the texts by referring to no. 115 (the Greeting for "Anointing Outside Mass") which leads the reader to no. 81 at the beginning of "Communion in Ordinary Circumstances"!

[10] "The circumstances of an emergency room or casualty ward of a hospital may make the proper celebration of the sacrament difficult. If the condition of the sick person does not make anointing urgent, the priest may find it better to wait for a more appropriate time to celebrate the sacrament."

[11] The reference is to the Appendix but is an incorrect number; it refers to no. 299, not 737 as mentioned.

[12] The translation is that of the *New Revised Standard Version* (New York: Oxford University Press, 1989).

[13] Daniel J. Harrington, "The Gospel According to Mark," *The New Jerome Biblical Commentary* (Englewood Cliffs, NJ: Prentice Hall, 1990) 597.

[14] Ibid.

[15] Robert Leaney, "Dominical Authority for the Ministry of Healing," *Expository Times* 65 (1953–54) 123.

[16] The section of James in question is inclusive of 5:13-16, although verses 14-15 are at the heart of the anointing of the sick. Some of the most recent relevant writings on the subject are Luke Timothy Johnson, *The Letter of James: A New Translation with Introduction and Commentary* (New York: Doubleday, 1995); Robert J. Karris, "Some New Angles on James 5:13-20," *Review and Expositor* 97 (2000) 207–19; Daniel R. Hayden, "Calling the Elders to Pray," *BSac* 138 (1981) 258–66; Bernhard Mayer, "Jak 5:13: ein Plaedoyer für das Bittgebet in der Kirche," *Dienst für den Menschen in Theologie und Verkündigung* (Regensburg: Friedrich Pustet, 1981) 165–78.

[17] Here the most obvious issue is the translation of the Greek *presbyteroi* (elders) as "priests" in Roman Catholic translations. For an in depth discussion, see John J. Ziegler, *Let Them Anoint the Sick* (Collegeville: Liturgical Press, 1987).

[18] In John 4:46-47; 11:1, 4, 14; Acts 9:37, it does imply serious sickness, but necessarily need not be limited to this.

[19] "The word *periculose* has been carefully studied and rendered as "seriously," rather than as "gravely," "dangerously," or "perilously." Such a rendering will serve to avoid restrictions upon the celebration of the sacrament. On the one hand, the sacrament may and should be given to anyone whose health is seriously impaired; on the other hand, it may not be given indiscriminately or to any person whose health is not seriously impaired."

[20] Charles Gusmer, *And You Visited Me: Sacramental Ministry to the Sick and the Dying*, rev. ed. (New York: Pueblo Publishing Company, 1989) 8.

[21] Ibid., 9.

[22] See also Canon 1007, 1983 Code of Canon Law.

[23] See n. 17 above.

[24] See also canon 1003, 1983 Code of Canon Law.

[25] Gusmer, *And You Visited Me*, 9.

[26] While the physical act of anointing someone with oil requires human touch (and therefore the laying on of hands is unavoidable), the formal development of a ritual "laying on of hands" seems to originate from an interpolation in the text added by Origen in his commentary, *On Leviticus* (Homily 2). See Gusmer, *And You Visited Me*, 9.

[27] See also Canon 999, 1983 Code of Canon Law.

[28] See Jeffrey John, "Anointing in the New Testament," *The Oil of Gladness: Anointing in the Christian Tradition*, ed. Martin Dudley and Geoffrey Rowell (London: SPCK, 1993) 46–76.

[29] See Gusmer, *And You Visited Me*, 9.

[30] Options B (for general use) and C (in extreme or terminal illness) seem most consistent with the widespread association of "Lord" with Jesus the Christ, historically and in contemporary theology. The christological underpinnings of much of anointing theology (with regard to the references to incarnation theology and a conforming to the suffering of Christ most prominently) make these prayers more consistent with the overall ritual action as much as they make the desire for physical healing more apparent.

[31] In the ninth-century Gregorian sacramentary (with the Hadrianum supplement), the priest was instructed to anoint the sick person "making a cross with sanctified oil, on the neck, on the throat, between the shoulders, on the chest, or where the pain is greatest" (Frederick S. Paxton, *Christianizing Death: The Creation of a Ritual Process in Early Medieval Europe* [Ithaca, NY: Cornell University Press, 1990] 151). The explanation of the Reunion Council of Florence (1439) provides an insight into anointings now treated as treatment of sinning senses: the sick person is "to be anointed on these parts: on the eyes on account of sight, on the ears on account of hearing, on the nostrils on account of smelling, on the mouth on account of taste and speech, on the hands on account of touch, on the feet on account of movement, on the loins on account of the lust seated there" (cited in Gusmer, *And You Visited Me*, 32). In the 1917 Code of Canon Law, the anointing of the loins was dropped.

[32] Gusmer, *And You Visited Me*, 9–10.

[33] See the description in Ziegler, *Let Them Anoint the Sick*, 31.

[34] Lathrop, *Holy Things*, 16.

[35] Ibid., 19.

[36] Ibid.

[37] Ibid., 18.

Chapter Two

The Threefold Ritual Center of Anointing of the Sick

Introduction

104. There are three distinct and integral aspects to the celebration of this sacrament: the prayer of faith, the laying on of hands, and the anointing with oil.

At the heart of the rite of the anointing of the sick are three ritual actions or "integral aspects" around which the sacramental rite is constructed. In the overview of the previous chapter, the fullness of the rite outside of Mass and within Mass were seen as preferred because they offered a liturgical context in which the richness of multiple interpretations could flourish. In the third form of the rite, "Anointing in a Hospital or Institution," the adaptations abbreviate the rite to accommodate the weak or very sick person, and in a situation of extreme urgency reduce the rite to the essential aspects of the prayer of faith, the laying on of hands, and the anointing with oil.

In this chapter we will explore each of these three essential components, first through biblical foundations, then in liturgical and ecclesiological usage, and finally in pastoral applications.

The Prayer of Faith

105. *Prayer of Faith:* The community, asking God's help for the sick, makes its prayer of faith in response to God's word and in a spirit of trust (see James 5:14-15). In the rites for the sick, it is the people of God who pray in faith. The entire Church is made present in this community—represented by at least the priest, family, friends, and others—assembled to pray for those to be anointed. If they are able, the sick persons should also join in this prayer.

Of the three primary components of the ritual that give flesh to the sacrament of the anointing of the sick, the first, the prayer of faith, receives the shortest explanation in the *praenotanda* and yet functions as the primary context for the description of anointing in the biblical letter of James. In a sense, both the laying on of hands and the anointing with oil are outward manifestations of the prayer of faith; it is all a prayer of faith, expressed in different ways. The contextualization of the laying on of hands and the anointing with oil within the prayer of faith is what sets the two physical actions apart from many other occasions of similar use in the larger society. In other words, anointing with oil has been part of many cultures and many religious traditions, but within the context of Christian prayer it has a spectrum of meanings that, while not uniform, are certainly more focused. The focusing lens is "in the name of the Lord" through which faith in the same Lord both encourages and makes efficacious this prayer of faith.

Within the field of liturgical theology, "context" as a liturgical construct can be understood in different ways. In Kevin Irwin's summary, context can mean "the historical evolution of a given liturgical rite" which gives insight into what it has meant to celebrate a particular ritual and how that is consistent with or at odds with what is understood today. It can also mean the methodology by which a contemporary rite is examined to "determine whether the contemporary celebration of these rites in specific contexts expresses what is actually envisioned in the published rites." Here the actual doing of the rite, with all its nonverbal communication needs to be observed, not just the texts on paper. Thirdly, Irwin describes context as a way to approach "the critical function of liturgical theology" with regard to "determining the adequacy of the present liturgical rites and of adapting them to a variety of changing ecclesial and cultural settings." Are these liturgical rites adequate to theological and ritual understandings?[1]

All of these are relevant to the prayer of faith, as well as to the other elements, in that inquiry into what they meant in the James text, what they meant throughout the history of the rite, and what they mean today are important, as well as contributing to the recognition of how the rite is received, understood, and celebrated in all of its possible variety. This will, in turn, contribute to a greater understanding of the three primary elements of the rite.

Biblical Foundations of the "Prayer of Faith"

The Letter of James is not alone in using the idea of the prayer of faith, and James clearly roots the concept in myriad references to faith in Scriptures and to the examples of Jesus' own healing as in the Gospels. But, in addition to the christological model, the Lukan example of boldness in asking God for assistance and the demonstrated faithfulness of those asking (Luke 11:9-10)[2] seems to be foundational to the three key verses of James (5:13-15) on which so much of the contemporary rite is based.

One of the hallmarks of prayer throughout the Letter of James is its association with wisdom: "the way to gain wisdom is prayer."[3] Wisdom, or the Spirit, gives the ones praying the discernment to know what to pray and, at the same time, works through those praying with divine power.[4] Applying this to the specific phrase, "the prayer of faith," which reads to one commentator like "a rubric from a Church order,"[5] bears out this "wisdom" tradition.[6] If it is encoded or "institutionalized," its key understandings are that what is efficacious is first God ("It is God's power which will heal the person")[7] and, by extension, the faithfulness of the one praying, so that a prayer of faith is one that "expresses trust in God and flows out of commitment to him, for only such prayers are effective."[8]

What is particular about the setting of prayer in James is that, unlike the individual, charismatic "pray-er" of Paul's letters (for example 1 Corinthians 12 and 14), the Spirit-filled efficacious prayer is that of the community as represented in the elders. The declaration that the sick will be saved "demonstrates the power of a righteous person's prayer. When the example is transferred to the Church, the righteous one cannot refer to an individual. Instead the prayer of the Church as a whole

serves the same purpose as the prayer of the prophet."⁹ The letter of
James calls the reader to the connection between the righteous Christian community praying and the efficacious prayer of the prophet by
concluding the section with a reminder of the effects of the prophet
Elijah's prayers (5:17-18).

This prayer of faith is done "over" *(epi)* the sick person, which implies "motion, figuratively or literally,"¹⁰ or physical closeness, literally,
above the person. Praying over someone might have a political as well
as a physical implication, so that to pray over the sick person was to assume praying with authority, the "collective authority" of those appointed by the community.¹¹

Finally, the prayer of faith is done "in the name of the Lord" which
also has numerous parallels with accounts of the disciples' ministry
(Mark 6:7-13; Matt 10:5-15; Luke 9:1-6; Acts 3:6-8). It is the "power of
Jesus Christ"¹² that makes concrete this sign of the reign of God. "This
practice indicates that in calling out the name the baptizer/healer/exor-
cist is acting as the representative of God calling upon the power of
God."¹³ In addition to "representing" God, the prayer removes any hint
of personal power and refers all who are present to the power of the
risen Lord. Interestingly, the example of these elders using the prayer
(and anointing) as vehicles "of strong estatic-pneumatic powers"¹⁴ is a
counter to the charge that James is not really a Christian epistle at all.
While the term and concept of elders was certainly an inheritance from
Judaism, "this exercise of eschatological power as a duty of office is
something not present in the synagogue elders."¹⁵ The juxtaposition of
this unusual action of the elders with "the name of the Lord" led one
Scripture scholar, Martin Dibelius, to two conclusions: a) this was a
Christian community; b) therefore the "Lord" equals "Jesus."¹⁶

The Liturgical Manifestation of the Prayer of Faith

The most frequent prayers for the sick throughout Christian history
have been the individual prayers of Christians for one another and for
all people. When we turn to liturgical prayer for the sick, the most frequent has probably been the inclusion of petitions for the sick in the
intercessory prayers of the Eucharist and the Liturgy of the Hours.
Whether the prayers functioned as litanies in the midst of the liturgy,
or as part of the eucharistic prayer proper,¹⁷ a remembrance for the sick
was one of the most constant features.¹⁸ These "Prayers of the Faithful"
were considered efficacious because of the Spirit, present in those pray-

ing and in the prayer act of the Church.[19] These were also prayers "in the name of the Lord," directed to the First Person of the Trinity in some traditions and to Christ in others. But the prayer of faith in the anointing of the sick implied a physical directness and, for many interpreters of the James passage, touch also, which made it a somewhat different genre of prayer than the intercessions of the gathered Church. Therefore, throughout the history of the anointing of the sick, prayer—in faith and in the name of the Lord—remained the context for the other elements involving touch (the laying on of hands) and the anointing (touch with oil), all of which contribute to the contemporary rite in practice and in understanding.

Within the contemporary rite of anointing of the sick, the prayer of faith is articulated in the ritual texts of the litany of intercession, the prayer of anointing[20] and the prayer after anointing. The litanies in both printed versions (121 and 138) are suggested, not fixed ("The priest may adapt or shorten the litany according to the condition of the sick person"), and are quite similar in focus in individual petitions. Interestingly enough, they are inversely structured from the model of general intercessions suggested for Mass. There, the intercessions begin with the broadest category and move to the narrower, or to individual concerns close at hand,[21] whereas the litany here moves from a focus on the individual sick person to those around him or her and then back to the individual (or group of individuals) on whom hands will be laid. Topically, the suggested petitions (121) pray for strength, freedom from all harm, freedom from sin and all temptation, relief from suffering, and then assistance to all who care for the sick (138 has a similar order but is worded more eloquently). So, the first articulation of the prayer of faith in the litany is focused on the sick person and addresses multiple dimensions of a Christian understanding of sickness. It is also the prayer that is most obviously the prayer of the gathered community in its ideal form. The ritual structure of the litany, with its recurring refrain of "Lord, have mercy" by all, articulates the "prayer of faith" as the community's prayer, the "action of the church,"[22] not just in words but by its very structure.

After the laying on of hands (in silence) and the acknowledgment of the blessed oil, the anointing formula itself continues the prayer of faith as articulated in the anointing rite. Here the inheritance of the James text is most apparent in the choice of phrases, particularly in the second half accompanying the anointing of hands: "May the Lord who frees you from sin save you and raise you up" (124). The complexity of psychosomatic efficacy is covered in short phrases faithfully echoing the language of James. It also echoes in the ears of those present and participating as integrated with the introduction of the rite, and models prayer based on biblical texts. This is prayer which speaks not just with christological and ecclesial efficacy, but also as the "axis" of continuing formation in prayer, drawing "primarily upon the Scripture" as stated in the rite's introduction to "Visits to the Sick" (55).[23]

The first half of the prayer of anointing also succinctly draws the sacramental action of the anointing into the words ("through this holy anointing") and articulates an epicletic dimension ("with the grace of the Holy Spirit") consistent with the formulae of other reformed sacraments. As with the scholarly debates over the entire James passage regarding the identity of "the Lord," this prayer also contains some ambiguity. Is the prayer referencing the First Person of the Trinity, here called "Lord," or is "Lord" equal to Jesus the Christ, confirming the incarnational aspects of the rite? A similar ambiguity of the effect of the anointing remains in the anointing formula also, criticized by some as lacking a "boldness" in praying for physical health and healing.[24]

The absent specificity is partially addressed in the third articulation of the "prayer of faith" in the rite, namely the "Prayer after Anointing." In the normative pattern of anointing outside Mass and also within the Eucharist, there are seven possible prayers to be used which immediately follow the anointing (although in the emergency rite of anointing in a hospital or other urgent situation, the prayer after anointing is separated from the actual anointing by the Lord's Prayer). The five options for adults are indicated as two for general use, one for extreme or terminal illness, one for advanced age, and one before surgery. The remaining two are for children, younger and older. The particular theological focus of each prayer differs in that they pick up a facet of the anointing formula fashioned from the James text. The first general prayer (125A) stresses "comfort in her suffering" with an emphasis on emotional strength and health ("when afraid," "when dejected," "when alone"). The second prayer (125B) strikes a balance between physical and spiritual healing ("cure the weakness of your servant") which is then explicated as healing the sickness and forgiving the sins, leading to "full health." The restoration of "former duties" is articulated as the goal. The third prayer (125C) has a quite different focus than the previous two, emphasizing the christological participation of the sick (and presumably, in many cases, dying) Christian, beginning with incarnational associations ("Lord Jesus Christ, you chose to share our human nature") and concluding with a reference to the passion ("Since you have given him a share in your own passion, help him to find hope in suffering"). This particular post-anointing prayer reflects in a more literal way than others the theology presented in the *praenotanda*. There, the initial introduction stresses the reality of sickness, suffering, and sin but through the Christian lens that all of these have meaning in Christ.[25] The fourth prayer option (125D) for the elderly articulates a difference between sickness and old age: getting old is not necessarily to be considered an illness, and instead focuses on "serenity in hope" and strength in weakness. In addition, there is a petition that the elderly person "may give us all an example of patience and joyfully witness to the power of your love," which is one of the few places where the prayers acknowledge what the sick do for us, rather than solely what the Church does for the sick.[26] The fifth prayer (125E), for those preparing for surgery, picks up another idea from paragraph 4 of the *praenotanda*, the cooperation between the medical arts and the healing ministry of the Church.[27] Here the prayer articulates that reality by acknowledging the hope that the divine grace of healing may come "through the skills of surgeons and nurses." This prayer contains a unique borrowing from the earliest prayers for healing that appeared as eucharistic embolisms towards the end of the first millennium, recalling the restoration of the sick person to the Church community as the "goal" of the healing ("May your servant respond to your healing will and be reunited with us at your altar of praise").[28]

Of the two children's prayers, the first (125F) uses simple language and concepts of protection ("Caress her, shelter her, and keep her in your tender care"), easily understood by both fearful parents and patients. The second (125G), written for older children, sits less easily, almost coming across as an ultimatum of required activity for the patients if they recover their health (". . . make him joyful in spirit, and ready to embrace your will").

Assessing the faithfulness of the intercessory prayer texts in the rite is not possible, as they are suggested outlines for litanies that would ideally vary in every situation. The fixed formula for the anointing of the sick and the seven options for the post-anointing prayer, however, honor both the inheritance from the James text and honestly reflect the history of the anointing of the sick in which different theologies were emphasized at different times and places in the historical rites. The anointing has not always been understood to have the same effect on the patient and on the gathered community. Therefore the prayers emerging from the tradition, particularly the post-anointing prayers, build on the ambiguity (or better, symbolic multivalence) of the anointing formula itself to concretize a particular theological dimension of the anointing and prayer that is most appropriate to the situation of the person being anointed. This seems most faithful to sacramental ideals, in that no sacrament exists in a generic, "cosmic" form, but rather that "sacramentality is profoundly temporal, profoundly spatial and profoundly relative."[29] This would, in turn, point to the need for perhaps several more options in the post-anointing prayer category, particularly to address situations that arise more and more frequently, such as additional prayers for long-term terminal illness and the common fear that one's individual sins have directly caused God's wrath to take the form of this particular illness.

In addition, the importance of the prayer of faith as the context for the whole sacramental act raises questions of liturgical meaning, not in text alone, but also in ritual structure. Is the verbal focusing of the anointing act better placed before or after the act itself if it functions as the "interpreter" of the action? The litanic prayer that leads in to the laying on of hands does seem to carry that weight, but it is not a fixed prayer like the anointing "prayers of faith." The *ordo* of liturgical structure has meaning in that the juxtaposition of elements one to another can change the meaning of the individual texts or actions. The arrangement of elements can help or hinder peoples' engagement in the multiple symbolic meanings of the anointing actions and prayers,[30] either by interpreting the elements in evocative ways, or by obscuring meanings that might have been intended and helpful.

Pastoral Practice and the Prayer of Faith

Overall, the set prayer texts present themselves as faithful to the theological introduction and intent of the overall rite and to the biblical and historical tradition that figures so prominently in the revised rituals. As with any liturgy, however, the prayer texts themselves are not the ritual; it is in the action of the "God who blesses" and in our "subsequent reaction"[31] of recognition and action that the sacrament occurs. As with many of the renewed rites, pastoral wisdom in making the best choices of texts and the nonverbal dimensions of the rite often take precedence in the comprehension and identification of the participants. This invites us to look at the other two key elements in the anointing of the sick: the laying on of hands and the anointing itself.

The Laying on of Hands in the Anointing of the Sick

106. *Laying on of hands:* The gospels contain a number of instances in which Jesus healed the sick by the laying on of hands or even by the simple gesture of touch. The ritual has restored to major significance the gesture of the laying on of hands with its several meanings. With this gesture the priest indicates that this particular person is the object of the Church's prayer of faith. The laying on of hands is clearly a sign of blessing, as we pray that by the power of God's healing grace the sick person may be restored to health or at least strengthened in time of illness. The laying on of hands is also an invocation: the Church prays for the coming of the Holy Spirit upon the sick person. Above all, it is the biblical gesture of healing and indeed Jesus' own usual manner of healing: "they brought the sick with various diseases to him; and he laid hands on every one of them and healed them" (Luke 4:40).

The laying on of hands is a recurring gesture in biblical descriptions and throughout Christian history. Its multiple associations, while rooted in common religious and cultural interpretations, develop out of and into variations on the twin foundations of transferal of power and blessing. In the rituals for the sick, the laying on of hands is one of the two primary outward manifestations of the prayer of faith. Along with the anointing with oil, the laying on of hands is a tangible expression of the relationship between the "pray-er" and God and between the human participants in the action of the Church and, like the anointing with oil, is a gesture shared with a broad range of sacramental rites.

Biblical Foundations of the Laying on of Hands

Unlike the prayer of faith and the anointing with oil which are explicitly mentioned in the key passage from James on which we are so dependent, the laying on of hands is more problematic for the simple reason that it is not there. The primary verses do not mention any laying on of hands, and its insertion into the interpretive tradition of James 5:13-15 seem to date from Origen (c. 250), who perhaps read the gesture into the text from his own experience of anointing the sick.[32] Regardless of its lack of overt rooting in the James text, the gesture does have broad biblical roots in a number of different contexts, including healing, and an extensively attested history of association with the anointing of the sick.

The laying on of hands as a biblically-based gesture has been the topic of a great deal of research and writing over the last century, particularly of concern for those writing on the efficacy and theology of ordination rites.[33] While many scholars have pointed out the continuity between understandings and uses of the laying on of hands in the Old and New Testaments, there are some notable differences in emphasis, too, particularly in the examples of Jesus and healing. Perhaps the watershed treatment for understanding the different Old Testament strands was David Daube's *The New Testament and Rabbinic Judaism*,[34] in which he distinguishes between two larger categories of contexts and meanings for the laying on of hands. The first, *samakh*, touching or, literally, "to lean upon," came to be associated with "the offering of sacrifice" (such as Lev 3:2, 8, 13) or in ordinations or consecrations (such as Num 8:10; Deut 34:9).[35] The second, *sim* or *shith*, "to place" or "touch," was associated with "an act of blessing."[36]

Daube's work was invaluable in pointing out the patterning of the Hebrew words and opening up the discussion for many insightful articles to follow. Later scholarship on ordination was divided in seeing the inheritance in the New Testament as primarily one of blessing or of the transferal of power, a distinction confused by the use of a single Greek term *(epitithui)* as translation for the several Hebrew concepts. Drawing a trajectory from the two strands of Old Testament tradition through the healing stories of the New Testament has also been problematic for some scholars because "the imposing of hands to effect healing . . . has no direct Old Testament counterpart."[37] The only precedent, if it may be called that, is a reference in one of the Dead Sea Scrolls, perhaps indicating an intertestamental Jewish practice.[38] One summary suggests a remote link between the resuscitation of a corpse in 2 Kings 13:21 *(naga)* and the healing touch of Jesus in the New Testament,[39] but to try and draw a direct precedent in the types of blessings by laying on of hands in the Old Testament with the descriptions of the acts of Jesus and the apostles in the New Testament is problematic.

> There is then no evidence that *sim* was ever used to indicate direct physical touch or imposition of hands in healing. Nor is there any reference in this way in the Talmud. It seems likely then that behind

the New Testament use of the imposition of hands in healing is not *sim* or *sit* as Daube postulates, but *naga*. This is supported in that in certain cases in the gospels there was no real imposition but simply a touching . . . in view of the fact that there is no direct precedent either in the Old Testament or in the Talmud for the use of the laying on of hands for healing, it would seem better to assume that the basic idea here is one of physical touch.[40]

The New Testament accounts of the gesture of laying on of hands are primarily focused on healings and blessings by Jesus and his followers, with a secondary emphasis on initiation and recognition of ministry. The number of dominical healings through touch constitutes the largest group (Matt 9:18; Mark 5:23; 6:5; 7:32; 8:23, 25) followed by dominical blessings of various kinds. The followers of Jesus also (and more specifically) used laying on of hands for healing (Mark 16:18; Acts 9:17; 28:8) for commissioning to ministry, and for initiation. While the accounts and the contexts are fairly clear in the New Testament stories, the interpretation of what they effected and what they mean for later ecclesial tradition is quite mixed. Again the focus has been on the use of laying on of hands (especially in Acts and the later Pastoral Epistles) as a prototype of ordination rites, and that focus of scholarship has carried over to the use of laying on of hands in New Testament healing accounts also. To that end, much of the assumption has been twofold: the gesture and its meaning has been borrowed directly from Jewish traditions laid out in the Old Testament; and because of that the laying on of hands causes conferral of the Spirit, or power, or authority.[41] J. Kevin Coyle cautions against overstating both assumptions, noting particularly that in both the Old and New Testaments, the so-called epicletic gesture is just as often confirming the recognition of the Spirit already present as it is bestowing the Spirit. Applied to the use of the gesture in healing, Coyle's argument supports and parallels the issue in a number of contemporary reflections on the anointing of the sick, which remind their readers that the sick have a prophetic role, and minister to others as much as they are ministered to through the sacramental actions of the Church.

Other scholars see the New Testament accounts of healing less as a gesture of recognition but as related to the transferal of power in ordination. In speaking of the stories of Jesus' healing in the Gospel of Mark, one scholar notes that "there seems to have been some transfer of power or of health in the healings, and this is the common interpretation of the laying on of hands."[42] Generally, the idea of blessing as a common umbrella of interpretive meaning which includes the transferal of power (because blessing is understood "as imparting something very definite")[43] is seen as the key to understanding the healing gesture of laying on of hands, both in the accounts of Jesus' healing and in those of his followers. In all cases, however, the gesture of laying on of hands as blessing is articulated by the verbal prayer to which it is joined, and is best understood as part of the "verb 'to bless' in the gospels."[44]

The multiple accounts of healing and blessing by Jesus and his followers in the New Testament, taken together as a whole, provide the basis for the ecclesial practice of continuing the gesture in healing rites, both by the prayer of faith in the name of Jesus, and in the gesture most used by Christ himself.

The Liturgical Manifestation of the Laying on of Hands

The brief summary above of the biblical foundation for the gesture of laying on of hands cannot help but return us to the description of those roots in paragraph 106 of the Introduction to the Anointing of the Sick. The carefully constructed description of the origins and meaning of this gesture there reflect the best of biblical scholarship while layering the theological meanings one on top of another (recognition, blessing, transferal of power, and epiclesis), in turn reflecting the organic history of the rite itself and this particular gesture.

The laying on of hands has been called a fundamental sacramental rite by which the Holy Spirit was brought back

> into the center, to the heart of the sacramental happening . . . it was done by either restoring or, as the case may be, highlighting the laying on of hands in the sacramental rites and also in blessings; *and* by making unmistakably clear in the accompanying documentation its intent to renew or strengthen the pneumatological understanding of the sacred rites.[45]

While we might quibble over the reduction of the laying on of hands to a solely epicletic interpretation, Diekmann's characterization of the laying of on hands as a basic sacramental building block has stood the test of time and scrutiny in many of the reformed rites, correcting centuries of a ritual pneumatological desert in Western Christian sacraments. The rites of initiation, the Eucharist, penance (ideally if not by implication when in a confessional), marriage, ordination, and anointing all have a laying on of hands as a central gesture.

In the anointing of the sick, the laying on of hands is placed between the litany and the anointing (or more specifically before the prayer over the oil or blessing) and done by putting both hands on the head of the sick person in silence (122, 139, 156, 247). After the prayer or blessing of oil, the second sacramental touch takes place in the form of the actual anointing. If we follow Diekmann's thesis that the action is interpreted by the accompanying words (faithful also to the official rite), a laying on of hands in silence must take its interpretation from the litany of prayer preceding it, as the remaining prayers focus on the anointing itself. The final petition of the litany "give life and health to your brother/sister N., on whom we lay our hands in your name" (121 and 138 for the first two contexts of anointing outside of and within Mass) summarizes the other petitions, particularly those focused on the sick individual(s), as well as the Scripture texts that preceded it. This invites the interpretation that the laying on of hands in this context is very much in continuity with what we saw of the actions of Jesus himself as recorded in the New Testament in which an element of divine power was transmitted, articulated in the stories that exemplify preaching the kingdom of God and doing the kingdom of God in healing.[46] The most directly related sequence of stories found in all three Synoptic Gospels is the "daughter of Jairus" story, framing that of the hemorrhaging woman. Both healings involve touch but, particularly in the story of the woman who reaches out and touches Jesus' clothes, we can see the central aspect of faith (the woman believes that the action of touching will indeed heal her) and the emanating of divine power (Jesus, "immediately aware that power had gone forth from him," wonders who has touched him [Mark 5:30]). "Give life and health to our brother/sister N., on whom we lay our hands in your name" continues this christological and incarnational proclamation of the reign of God.

Turning to the rubrics of the laying on of hands, why does silence, rather than spoken prayer, accompany the gesture? A number of factors may contribute to the choice to stop talking and let the gesture itself speak. The first factor may simply be the power of good ritual; silence heightens the solemnity of the action as it grabs our attention. There is nothing that can make us more aware of each other than being in silence together and, as the laying on of hands is mediated through the very tangible experience of human touch, it is communicating relationality, human to human, human community to individual, and divine to human. Historically, there is a possible precedent for silence in the sequence of rubrics at the laying on of hands in the early Church document Apostolic

Tradition whose second to fourth century compilation of liturgical *or-dines* has become the basis for so many of the renewed liturgical texts and actions of the twentieth century.[47] At the description of episcopal ordination, the Latin text says

> When all give consent, let them lay hands on him, and let the pres-bytery stand by, being still. And let all keep silence, praying in their heart for the descent of the Spirit.[48]

The silence allows all to equally "pray" in their own mental images or words for the one identified as the primary recipient of the prayer at that moment. Oddly enough, this seems a contradiction to the idea that the written and thus spoken prayers always interpret the ritual and sacramental gestures. Here the silence allows for any number of prayers to accompany and therefore "interpret" the action.

The most thoughtful reflection on silence in recent sacramental theological writings may be that of David Power. He describes language as the "expression of intent . . . to bring to humans the gift and the invitation into a communion that transcends the limits of the particular. Hence, of its nature language has a horizon beyond the percep-tions which it itself voices."[49] Because the goal of language, therefore, is to reach beyond what it is capable of achieving,

> humans need the times of silence for two reasons. First, they need to gather in what language says and to reflect upon it. Second, they need the silence to be in touch with the intent of language which is beyond itself, and thus in touch with the intent of the heart which opens up horizons beyond the expressions of whatever language has brought to expression and to being. It might almost be said that lan-guage brings us into silence.[50]

In the anointing of the sick, this movement into silence from language is concretized in the moment of the laying on of hands, in which the gesture stands for our prayers, spoken and unspoken and beyond our ability to ask, for the healing of this individual or group of individuals. The centrality of this gesture was historically attested to by the name given to the overall rite for the sick in ninth-century Milan, *Impositio manuum super infirmum*.[51]

The rubric of laying on of hands on the head is also worth noting. In all the sacramental rites, the laying on of hands is differentiated from touch by its two-handed application and the preferred placement on the body, namely on the head. The preference for the head, which historically, socially, and ritually has signified the crown of the person or the symbolic "responsible party" for the psychosomatic whole,[52] is the receiving point for the hands, which have historically, socially, and ritually represented the whole action or intent of God or of an individual messenger/disciple of God.[53] The gesture of touching on the head, with its extensive biblical and historical layers of meaning, is also a visual and gestural link to the other sacraments, which makes for interesting interpretive possibilities regarding the restored epicletic gesture of the Eucharistic Prayer.

Pastoral Practice and the Laying on of Hands

In 1989 Charles Gusmer wrote that "the laying on of hands is no longer an afterthought appended to the prayer of exorcism, but is an integral sacramental action to be performed by the priests (presbyters) in silence . . . its place in the rite of anointing should be better appreciated."[54] What Gusmer and others argued was that the silent gesture calls for an integrity of intention and duration in order to allow all present to "pray in their hearts" for the life and health of this individual.

Not only does the ritual gesture demand a ritual focus that clears the rite of inappropriate speed and busyness, but the reality of human touch, one of the last human senses we are capable of knowing when dying, is at the incarnational heart of the mediation of this multivalent symbolic action. Particularly when one is sick and/or under heavy medication, the senses are slower to react than during times of health. This sacramental touch communicates the self-communication of God and the web of relationships through that communication. It also calls forth the response of faith in the sick person and all who are gathered around. Because of this, the laying on of hands is a particularly important moment in which both its commonality with all good human touch is exploited and its fundamental difference from ordinary human touch is celebrated.

Anointing with Oil

107. *Anointing with Oil:* The practice of anointing the sick with oil
    signifies healing, strengthening, and the presence of the Spirit.

In the Gospel of Mark the disciples were sent out by the Lord to continue his healing ministry: "They anointed many sick people with oil and cured them" (Mark 6:13). And Saint James witnesses to the fact that the Church continued to anoint the sick with oil as both a means and a sign of healing (James 5:14). The Church's use of oil for healing is closely related to its remedial use in soothing and comforting the sick and in restoring the tired and the weak. Thus the sick person is strengthened to fight against the physically and spiritually debilitating effects of illness. The prayer for blessing the oil of the sick reminds us, furthermore, that the oil of anointing is the sacramental sign of the presence, power, and grace of the Holy Spirit.

If the anointing is to be an effective sacramental symbol, there should be a generous use of oil so that it will be seen and felt by the sick person as a sign of the Spirit's healing and strengthening presence. For the same reason, it is not desirable to wipe off the oil after the anointing.

The third fundamental ritual element of anointing of the sick is the actual anointing with oil itself. Both biblically and historically, anointing with oil has remained at the heart of the ritual, but it is the physical, social, political, and economic associations of anointing with oil that often set it apart from the prayer of faith and the laying on of hands. While all three of these elements have parallels outside of Christian history, the volume of information about the importance of oil and anointings throughout Mediterranean cultures has made it a topic of comparative studies to a far greater extent. Within the liturgical history of anointing of the sick, the application of blessed oil in the name of the Lord has remained the central action, frequently lending its name to the overall orchestration of rituals and words that have variously made up the rite throughout history. In addition, the anointing with oil, like the prayer of faith and the laying on of hands, links the anointing of the sick with other sacramental rites, particularly initiation and ordination (and at various points in Christian history, marriage and death).

As with the other two primary ritual elements, the biblical roots of anointing of the sick are rich and varied, especially in Old Testament traditions. While the use of oil is far more limited in use in the New Testament, much of the rich imagery of the Old Testament is carried forward in the writers of the early Church, particularly those from the eastern part of the Mediterranean basin.

Biblical Foundations of the Anointing with Oil

Scholars have noted three different types of oil described in the writings of the Old Testament, in addition to multiple uses for each of the three types. The first type was one of the "first fruits," called *yishar*," usually referring to the best of the new oil from the first press "produced by treading out the newly picked olives (Deut 18:4)."[55]

The second word for oil in the Old Testament is *sĕmen*. Compared to the first type, "This was oil of inferior quality, produced in larger quantities by repeated pressing of the olive pulp, but the word comes to be a general term for oil in the Bible."[56] *Sĕmen*, in spite of its pedestrian association, was often linked to health through its use as a "basic food" (Eccl 39:26) or external application for skin care (Ps 104:15). Because of its literal link to strength and health, it was a direct symbolic leap to seeing this oil as associated with strengthening humans through healing. Oil itself, or oil in combination with other ingredients, was a natural "mendicament for the soothing of wounds (Isa 1:6)"[57] as well as an applied symbol for related realities such as reconciliation (Mic 6:15) and for joyful social events (Amos 6:6). It is particularly in the *Pseudepigrapha* that the images of anointing for healing are developed.[58]

The third type of oil was actually the *sĕmen* with spices and ingredients added that made it an ointment, called *roqah*. "Its use was strictly confined to certain ritual purposes: a layperson was forbidden to make it or to apply it to the human body on pain of death (Exod 30:32-33)."[59] This latter oil was used for anointing places and things (Exod 30:26-28) and the high priest (Lev 8:12). "The purpose of anointing was to 'make holy' or to 'consecrate,' in the case of cultic impedimenta."[60] This consecration effected two results: first the recipient received "a particular character" and second, the recipient was set apart "from the circumstances of ordinary human life."[61] The high priest (and members of the priestly caste) and the king were the most frequent recipients of this consecratory anointing in the writings of the Old Testament and represent two different strands of this tradition,[62] but both created or acknowledged a more profound relationship with God, drawing the one anointed into a deeper or more particular participation with the divine.

Compared to the multitude of references to oil and anointings in the Old Testament, the New Testament has very few. While some scholars see intimations of initiatory chrismations in some passages,[63] there are really only two passages with "obvious bearing on the Church's practice of sacramental anointing":[64] Mark 6:13 and James 5:14-15. These are dependent on the religious, cultural, and medicinal associations of oil, but both go beyond simply presenting oil as a medicine alone. "Healing is not effected by the oil as a medicine, but by the oil applied along with prayer and the pronouncing of the name.[65] It is the context as described above in the section on the prayer of faith, into which divine power and ecclesial intent are mediated through the touch and application of oil, that effects this healing. "Thus [the anointing in James] is either the outward sign of the inward power of prayer, or, more likely, a sacramental vehicle of divine power as in Mark 6:13."[66] Biblical scholarship has more recently tended against seeing the anointing in James as a solely medicinal or magical application of oil in keeping with an earlier Jewish concern for limiting the ritual use of oil.[67] This is consistent with the larger scholarly movement away from using a solely sociological or natural perspective, in this case seeing the anointing solely from the perspective of the healing properties of oil itself (" . . . the function of oil in James is not medicinal except insofar as it partakes of the eschatological oils")[68] and toward a differentiation of medicinal and sacramental applications of oil in contemporary rites.[69] Certainly in the time of Mark and James, however, the eschatological meaning of oil, the mediation of "messianic power" in Mark 6:13,[70] the "power and authorization of the community's post-Easter activity,"[71] the use of oil as "metaphorical of divine blessing,"[72] and other meanings associated with anointing were all enriched and grounded in the natural and cultural associations that oil already had in its multiple daily usage. Ricoeur's "symbol gives rise to thought" is dependent here as everywhere on the first level meaning of symbolic discourse being humanly accessible and tangible.[73]

The immediate biblical roots of the developed sacramental rite of anointing with oil are thus in this single Markan passage and the subsequent description in James. One of the primary ritual developments surrounding the oil and its use in healing is the addition of a discreet and distinct blessing for the oil. The oil used is not just oil, nor is it blessed in its use in the historical development of the rite; rather the specific preparation of this oil through blessing will carry the ecclesial character of the anointing in many geographical areas and in particular historical periods in ways not present in the New Testament biblical passages.

The Liturgical Manifestation of the Anointing with Oil

There are two primary ritual components of the anointing with oil within the anointing of the sick. The first, "Prayer over the Oil" (123, 140, 157 with reference to number 20 in the "Blessings of Oils and Chrism") contains two options, either a "prayer of thanksgiving over blessed oil" (123) or a "blessing of oil," and the second, the actual anointing (124, 141, 157) with simple rubrics and the formula for anointing.

The description of the necessary oil itself in the *praenotanda* (20–25) contains more information on the anointing and the oil, beginning with the preference for olive oil, and only in particular circumstances (geographical, cultural, issues of accessibility) "other oil derived from plants" (20). The same introduction states the preference for the use of oil "blessed for this purpose by the bishop or by a priest who has the faculty," concluding with the statement that the "oil of the sick is ordinarily blessed by the bishop on Holy Thursday" (21), which is reflected in the primary ritual position given to the thanksgiving over oil already blessed. The thanksgiving is a set text ("if the oil is already blessed, the priest says the following prayer of thanksgiving over it" [123]) and presented in the format of a solemn blessing in which the gathered family, friends, and sick person respond to three acclamations with "blessed be God who heals us in Christ." The acclamations, trinitarian in scope, praise God who first "sent your Son to live among us and bring us salvation," who "humbled yourself to share in our humanity and . . . heal our infirmities," and whose "unfailing power gives us strength in our bodily weakness." These three acclamations are followed by the concluding petition, "God of mercy, ease the sufferings and comfort the weakness of your servant N., whom the Church anoints with this holy oil," which sets up a parallel with the conclusion of the litany of prayer ("Give life and health to your brother/sister N., on whom we lay our hands in your name."). This final acclamation points directly to the ritual action of the anointing which follows.

The alternative blessing of oil, permitted when the one anointing is equated "with diocesan bishops" or "in case of necessity, any priest, but only within the celebration of the sacrament" (21) is an addition in this *editio typica*. Drawing on images from the "Blessing of the Oil of the Sick" in the Chrism Mass, the first "Blessing of Oil" in the normative "Anointing Outside Mass" is an epiclesis over the oil with an

expansive description of the physical properties of oil reminiscent of
fourth-century prayers:

> God of all consolation,
> you chose and sent your Son to heal the world.
> Graciously listen to our prayer of faith:
> send the power of your Holy Spirit, the Consoler,
> into this precious oil, this soothing ointment,
> this rich gift, this fruit of the earth.
>
> Bless this oil ✠ and sanctify it for our use.
>
> Make this oil a remedy for all who are anointed with it;
> heal them in body, in soul, and in spirit,
> and deliver them from every affliction.
>
> We ask this through our Lord Jesus Christ, your Son,
> who lives and reigns with you and the Holy Spirit,
> one God, for ever and ever. Amen.

The blessing of oil in "Anointing within Mass" is modeled on the
"Thanksgiving over Blessed Oil" with the same refrain ("Blessed be
God who heals us in Christ") and a rather vague epiclesis at the conclu-
sion ("Almighty God, come to our aid and sanctify this oil . . ." 140).
In the introductory paragraph on anointing with oil (107) the prayer for
the blessing of oil is presented as a reminder "that the oil of anointing
is the sacramental sign of the presence, power, and grace of the Holy
Spirit," an interesting interpretation of the historical association of oil
which traditionally symbolized the incarnate messianic power of the
Second Person of the Trinity, rather than this emphasis on the Third
Person of the Trinity.

The anointing itself is accompanied by a new formula:

> Through this holy anointing may the Lord in his love and mercy
> help you with the grace of the Holy Spirit. Amen. May the Lord
> who frees you from sin save you and raise you up. Amen. (25)

Both in the introduction and in the rite itself (124) the formula is divided into two parts: the first phrase accompanies the anointing of the
forehead and the second the anointing of the hands. Both the rite and
the introduction make allowances for cultural sensitivities, particularly
those involving culturally defined, inappropriate touch, and for medical
adaptations (changing the placement of the anointing and the number
of anointings). There are no rubrical instructions within the rite itself
on how the anointing is done; it is only in ancillary commentaries that

additional instructions are included which link the anointing to earlier practices, particularly with regard to anointing in the form of a cross, anointing with the right thumb, and anointing on either the palms or the back of the hands, depending on the recipient's ordained status.

Pastoral Practice and the Anointing with Oil

Of the three primary ritual elements in the anointing of the sick, only the anointing with oil has a pastoral guideline added to its essential summary paragraph in the anointing of the sick instruction, reflecting the changed ritual instructions. Because of the difficulty many priests trained within a more minimalist use of sacramental matter have in changing gears, this instruction returns the "matter of the sacrament" (oil) to a primary place, in recognition of the importance of the ritual substance and action, not just the verbal formulae.

> If the anointing is to be an effective sacramental symbol, there should be a generous use of oil so that it will be seen and felt by the sick person as a sign of the Spirit's healing and strengthening presence. For the same reason, it is not desirable to wipe off the oil after the anointing (107).

Oil that "will be seen and felt" lends itself to bridging the medicinal, cultural, and sacramental understandings of this substance. The rite seems to beg for a slower, more engaged use of touch to communicate presence, not only divine to human but also human to human. The very stuff of the sacrament is one place where the rite reflects a sense of developing liturgy. Here an older approach that emphasized a particular sacramental moment separated from the larger arena of care of the sick, and the even larger arena of medicinal and cultural care for the sick, is juxtaposed with a more organic and integrated approach to sacrament rooted in the meeting of human and divine through the stuff of a good and bountiful creation.

Conclusion

The three primary elements of the anointing of the sick described above: the prayer of faith, the laying on of hands, and the anointing with oil, have formed an interwoven core of ritual prayer, spoken and acted, through much of Christian history. The contemporary rites within Pastoral Care of the Sick (PCS) have restored the balance between the elements and articulated their scriptural roots and longer historical tradition in much clearer ways than the immediate ritual predecessor of extreme unction.

Each of these elements, however, also raises questions about who is doing what and what is being effected by these actions, particularly when the rite is done in different circumstances and with different secondary elements. In the next chapter we will explore some of the theological issues surrounding these questions, reflecting less on how the rite is done or from where the individual elements were drawn, and more on what it means to do the rite, who can do what parts of the rite, and who is the appropriate recipient of the anointing of the sick.

Notes, Chapter Two

[1] Kevin Irwin, *Context and Text: Method in Liturgical Theology* (Collegeville: Liturgical Press, 1994) 54–55.

[2] "So I say to you, ask, and it will be given you; search, and you will find; knock, and the door will be opened for you. For everyone who asks receives, and everyone who searches finds, and for everyone who knocks, the door will be opened." The similarity of the literary structure of James with this and Paul's section in 1 Corinthians 7:18, 21, 27, has caught the attention of several exegetes. See particularly Peter H. Davids, *The Epistle of James: A Commentary on the Greek Text* (Grand Rapids, MI: Eerdmans Pub. Co., 1982) 56–57. In addition, biblical scholars note the similarities or prayer descriptions with Matthew 18:1-20; 21:22; Mark 11:24; John 14:13-14; 15:7; 16:23 (again, see Davids, 56).

[3] Ibid., 56.

[4] Ibid., 57.

[5] E. M. Sidebottom, *James, Jude and 2 Peter* (London: Thomas Nelson & Sons, Ltd, 1967) 62.

[6] Not only does "the prayer of faith" seem to be a code phrase for the description of wisdom's methodological and efficacious dimensions, but the phrase is a unicum within the New Testament. See Edouard Cothenet, "Healing as a Sign of the Kingdom, and the Anointing of the Sick," *Temple of the Holy Spirit: Sickness and Death of the Christian in the Liturgy* (New York: Pueblo Pub. Co., 1983) 43.

[7] Davids, *The Epistle of James,* 57.

[8] Ibid., 194.

[9] Pheme Perkins, *First and Second Peter, James, and Jude* (Louisville: John Knox Press, 1995) 92.

[10] J. Harold Greenlee, *An Exegetical Summary of James* (Dallas: Summer Institute of Linguistics, Inc., 1993) 222.

[11] Robert W. Wall, *Community of the Wise: The Letter of James* (Valley Forge, PA: Trinity Press International, 1997) 265.

[12] Cothenet, "Healings as a Sign of the Kingdom," 42.

[13] Davids, *The Epistle of James*, 193.

[14] Martin Dibelius, *James: A Commentary on the Epistle of James*, trans. Michael A. Williams, ed. Helmut Koester (Philadelphia: Fortress Press, 1976) 253.

[15] Davids, *The Epistle of James*, 194.

[16] Dibelius, *James*, 253.

[17] For the history and structuring of these prayers, see Paul De Clerck, *La "prière universelle" dans les liturgies latines anciennes. Témoignages patristiques et texts liturgiques*: LQF 62 (Münster: Aschendorff, 1977).

[18] A summary of the topics of the intercessions in historic liturgies is given in W. Jardine Grisbrooke's "Intercession at the Eucharist: 1. The Intercession at the Synaxis" in *Studia Liturgica IV* (1965) 133–41.

[19] This is also apparently the reason for their restriction to the baptized in a number of early Church texts; the catechumens were not yet filled with the Spirit and were unable to participate in these ecclesiologically efficacious prayers. "Henceforth they will pray with the rest of the people, for they do not pray with the faithful before obtaining all this" (*Traditio apostolica* 21 [Botte's translation, 54–55; cited]. Cited in Robert Cabié, "The General Intercessions or Prayer of the Faithful" in *The Church at Prayer, Volume II: The Eucharist* [Collegeville: Liturgical Press, 1986] 69).

[20] See Gusmer, *And You Visited Me*, 189.

[21] 1982 GIRM, #46, General Intercessions. "As a rule the sequence of intentions is to be: a. for the needs of the Church; b. for public authorities and the salvation of the world; c. for those oppressed by any need; d. for the local community."

[22] See Gusmer, *And You Visited Me*, see p. 190, for a discussion on prayer.

[23] Mary Collins, "The Roman Ritual: Pastoral Care and Anointing of the Sick," *Pastoral Care of the Sick: Concilium* 1991/2 (Philadelphia: Trinity Press, 1991) 5.

[24] Ibid., 10.

[25] *General Introduction: Human Sickness and its Meaning in the Mystery of Salvation*, particularly paragraphs 1–3.

[26] For a fuller presentation of this theology of the sick and for the differentiation between old age and sickness per se, see James L., *Empereur, Prophetic Anointing: God's Call to the Sick, the Elderly and the Dying* (Wilmington, DE: Michael Glazier, 1982).

[27] "The sick person is not the only one who should fight against illness. Doctors and all who are devoted in any way to caring for the sick should consider it their duty to use all the means which in their judgment may help the sick, both physically and spiritually" (ibid., 4).

[28] These types of prayers are found particularly in the prayers of the Vatican Gelasian texts and in the Bobbio Missal. Antoine Chavasse regards all the prayers as Roman in origin, although they appear in the mixed Roman–Gallican texts of the eighth century. See Antoine Chavasse, "Le sacramentaire gélasien (Vatican

Reginensis 316): Sacramentaire presbytéral en usage dans les titre romains au vii siècle." *Bibliothèque de théologie*, Ser. 4, vol. I (Paris, 1958) 460–61.

[29] Kenan Osborne, *Christian Sacraments in a Postmodern World: A Theology for the Third Millennium* (New York: Paulist Press, 1999) 70.

[30] See Gordon Lathrop, *Holy Things: A Liturgical Theology* (Minneapolis: Fortress Press, 1993) for a more complete argument on *ordo*.

[31] Ibid., pp. 74–75.

[32] " . . . in the remission of sins through penitence that which James the Apostle says, 'if someone is sick, let him call the elders of the church *and let them lay their hands upon him*, anointing him with oil in the name of the Lord" (Origen, Hom in Lev 2.4, cited in Dibelius, *James*, 252, n. 61).

[33] See Susan K. Woods, *Sacramental Orders* (Collegeville: Liturgical Press, 2000) especially ch. 2; Thomas P. Rausch, "Priestly Identity: Priority of Representation and the Iconic Argument," *Worship* 73 (1999) 69–79; James F. Puglisi, *The Process of Admission to Ordained Ministry: Epistemological Principles and Roman Catholic Rites*, vol. I, trans. Michael S. Driscoll and Mary Misrahi (Collegeville: Liturgical Press, 1996); and Everett Ferguson, "Laying on of Hands: Its Significance in Ordination," *JTS* 26 (1975) 2–10.

[34] London: The Athlone Press, 1956.

[35] Ibid., 225.

[36] Ibid., 227 (see the contrast of both of these categories of meanings, however, in Genesis 48:14ff.).

[37] J. K. Parratt, "The Laying on of Hands in the New Testament," *Expository Times* 80 (1968–69) 210.

[38] Genesis Apocryphon, col. xx, lines 16–29; J. A. Fitzmyer, *The Genesis Apocryphon of Qumran, Cave 1. A Commentary* (Rome, 1966).

[39] Parratt, "The Laying on of Hands," 212.

[40] Ibid.

[41] J. Kevin Coyle, "The Laying on of Hands as Conferral of the Spirit: Some Problems and a Possible Solution," *Studia Patristica* 18 (1983) 339.

[42] Ferguson "Laying on of Hands," 2.

[43] Ibid.

[44] Ibid., 4.

[45] Godfrey Diekmann, "The Laying on of Hands: The Basic Sacramental Rite," *CTSA Proceedings* 29 (1974) 349–50.

[46] Ibid., see especially pp. 9–10.

[47] The most recent and comprehensive edition is by Paul F. Bradshaw, Maxwell E. Johnson, and L. Edward Phillips, *The Apostolic Tradition: A Commentary*, ed. Harold W. Attridge (Minneapolis: Fortress Press, 2002). See especially pp. 24–29.

[48] Ibid., 24.

[49] David Power, *Sacrament: The Language of God's Giving* (New York: Crossroads Publishing Co., 1999) 73.

[50] Ibid., 74.

[51] Gusmer, *And You Visited Me*, 164.

[52] Unlike contemporary associations of head with intellect, biblical literature metaphorically links head with "center," "source," "authority," "center of person." The forehead as the place of shame (particularly in North African Christianity) is tied to its being the center of consciousness also. Most biblical dictionaries trace this association and its link to ecclesial sacramental actions.

[53] Diekmann, "The Laying on of Hands," 349–50; Lizette Larson-Miller, "Handing the Bread and Cup," *Assembly* 25 (1999) 36–37.

[54] Gusmer, *And You Visited Me,* 73.

[55] J. Roy Porter, "Oil in the Old Testament," *Oil of Gladness: Anointing in the Christian Tradition*, ed. Martin Dudley and Geoffrey Rowell (London: SPCK, 1993) 35.

[56] Ibid., 36.

[57] Ibid., 41.

[58] Ibid.

[59] Ibid.

[60] Ibid., 36–37.

[61] Ibid.

[62] Ibid., 38. Porter is careful to note that these two anointings (kingly and priestly) were actually two different rites. Quoting Giovanni Garbini, he notes that "royal anointing materially sanctions a designation already made or a quality already possessed, whereas priestly anointing 'itself confers a particular quality'. . . the king is anointed because he is king; the priest becomes priest by virtue of being anointed."

[63] See the introduction to Jeffrey John, "Anointing in the New Testament," *The Oil of Gladness,* 46.

[64] Ibid.

[65] Dibelius, *James,* 252.

[66] Davids, *The Epistle of James,* 193.

[67] James B. Adamson, *The Epistle of James* (Grand Rapids, MI: Eerdmans, 1976) 197.

[68] Davids, *The Epistle of James,* 193.

[69] See the documentation of the rite itself, particularly paragraph 107, and more recent cautionary writings about the different types and efficacies of anointing.

[70] Wall, *The Community of the Wise,* 265.

[71] Ibid., 266.

[72] Ibid., 265.

[73] See Paul Ricoeur, "The Symbol Gives Rise to Thought," *The Symbolism of Evil,* trans. Emerson Buchanan (New York: Harper & Row Pub., 1967) 347–57.

Chapter Three

Theological Questions from the Rite

P rior to the Second Vatican Council and continuing afterwards as the liturgical fruits of the council began to emerge, a number of theological questions emerged from discussions on the whole issue of pastoral care of the sick and eventually from the proposed rite for anointing of the sick. They were questions that looked both at historical continuity between what earlier councils had said about the meaning of the rite and how the contemporary rite was reflecting or moving beyond incorporating elements of that historical trajectory. In some cases the tensions that gave rise to productive and engaging discussions were based on pastoral needs that found themselves at odds with current practices. In other cases real theological differences emerged at both the roots of issues and in the ritual results of those roots. The questions are usually grouped under four categories: matter and form, the minister, the subject, and the effects. These "classic" issues have been well explored by a number of writers, most thoroughly by David Power,[1] but also with regard to specific elements by Jennifer Glen,[2] John Ziegler,[3] John Huels,[4] and most recently, by a number of authors at an international symposium on Pastoral Care of the Sick, sponsored by The National Association of Catholic Chaplains.[5]

This chapter gathers together current discussions in both theological and pastoral circles to summarize where these four issues, which have been part of the discussion before, during, and after Vatican Council II, now stand, and where the remaining questions in dialogue with the actual doing of the rite may lead in future discussions. Each section begins with a summary of the related paragraphs from the General Introduction to the Pastoral Care of the Sick.

A. The Matter and Form of the Rite

20. The matter proper for the sacrament is olive oil or, according to circumstances, other oil derived from plants.

21. The oil used for the anointing of the sick must be blessed for this purpose by the bishop or a priest who has faculty, either from the law or by special concession of the Apostolic See.

    The law itself permits the following, besides a bishop, to bless the oil of the sick:
    a) those whom the law equates with diocesan bishops;
    b) in case of necessity, any priest, but only within the celebration of the sacrament.

    The oil of the sick is ordinarily blessed by the bishop on Holy Thursday.

22. If a priest in accord with no. 21b, is to bless the oil during the rite, he may bring the unblessed oil with him, or the family of the sick person may prepare the oil in a suitable vessel. If any of the oil is left after the celebration of the sacrament, it should be absorbed in cotton (cotton wool) and burned.

    If the priest uses oil that has already been blessed (either by the bishop or by a priest), he brings it with him in the vessel in which it is kept. This vessel, made of suitable material, should be clean and should contain sufficient oil (soaked in cotton [cotton wool] for convenience). In this case, after celebrating the sacrament the priest returns the vessel to the place where it is kept with proper respect. He should make sure that the oil remains fit for use and should replenish it from time to time, either yearly when the bishop blesses the oil on Holy Thursday or more frequently if necessary.

25. The following is the sacramental form with which the anointing of the sick is given in the Latin rite:

    Through this holy anointing
    may the Lord in his love and mercy help you
    with the grace of the Holy Spirit.

> May the Lord who frees you from sin
> save you and raise you up.

The "stuff" of anointing, oil, has been discussed above in Chapter Two with regard to its cultural, historical, and theological associations. Paragraph 20 of the General Introduction addresses the type of oil to be used but makes exception for cultures and other areas of the world where pure olive oil may not be available. While this in itself became a topic of discussion because of the root issue of inculturation (whether the unity and efficacy of the rite is held together by a unity of material things and the same words/language or by their dynamic equivalent in meaning), the more compelling and far-reaching issue has been the introduction of an alternative blessing option as described in paragraphs 21 and 22 of the General Introduction. The labored explanations point to the novelty of this change, but beneath it all lies the deeper issue of liturgical tradition, of how the episcopacy represents the Church, of ecclesiology in general, and therefore of sacramentality.

Part of the difficulty in trying to summarize changes in the rites and their subsequent implications is that the historical continuity of any given rite, and especially of the anointing of the sick, cannot be taken for granted or oversimplified. The assumptions and practices regarding anointing of the sick in the first millennium of Christianity are not the same as those in the second millennium, which makes taking one issue and seeing it through the entire history without reference to other circumstances deceptive, to say the least. In light of that fact, the key issue with the "matter" of the sacrament—oil—is not so much the physical properties of the oil but its spiritual properties as blessed oil.[6] There is a long tradition, dating at least from the fourth and fifth centuries in some places, of using oil blessed by the bishop.[7] Whether that oil was used in a domestic setting by baptized lay Christians, or by priests, deacons, widows, bishops, or others sent out to anoint the sick or to receive the sick at the church, the episcopal blessing of oil was a way of expressing ecclesial representation, as was the presence of the one doing the anointing, the one being anointed, and those gathered to pray for the sick. The oil was itself sign—sacrament—of the living and active presence of Christ in the world through the ministry of the Church.[8] In other words, "the one common factor" in many of these various anointing tracks was the blessing of the oil by the bishop.[9]

One notable exception, often unrecognized in writings on the anointing of the sick, was the alternative to the bishop found in the martyrs, and later in the more broadly defined category of saints. Martyrs in particular stood for the Church and represented it, both locally and universally, in a parallel way to bishops. They had died, not for themselves, but to glorify God and for the building up of the Church to further the reign of God. Following that theology and the almost universal early Christian belief that the martyrs, by their immediate presence before the face of God, bridged heaven and earth,[10] oil could be blessed by its contact with the tomb of a martyr. This was done most frequently by pouring the oil through the tomb of the dead and collecting it from a spout on the bottom created for this purpose.[11] From there it could be taken home and used as needed or used *in situ* at healing services on the feast day of the martyr. While this tradition was more prevalent in the eastern regions of the Church, it was also found in the Western Church.[12] What is different in the West, however, was the establishment of a balance of power between the saints and the bishops, with the bishops of the Latin-speaking church asserting their control over the holy sites and therefore over what took place at the saints' tombs, a phenomenon masterfully described by Peter Brown in his study on saints in the Western tradition.[13] The story of St. Genevieve and the blessing of oil, told in the ninth century and then again in the eleventh century, exemplifies the solidification of the bishop's role as sole human agent of the sanctification of the oil for the sick. In the earlier version of the story, Genevieve herself blesses the oil as requested, producing the necessary efficacious results to heal the sick. In the second telling of the story, after praying, she refers the request to the bishop, who finishes the blessing of the oil, making the healing efficacious.[14]

The liturgical texts themselves, however, point to more exceptions, or at least to a more mixed history than the secondary descriptions of the tradition often allow. In the earliest of the sacramentaries representing the mixed Roman-Gallican tradition, in the *ordines* of the Roman and mixed traditions, and in the slightly later pontificals, the blessing of the oil of the sick is not always clearly reserved to the bishop. The consecration or blessing of all the oils at the chrismal Mass by the bishop alone appears in the tenth century Romano-Germanic pontificals.[15] This Mass, fixed in the second millennium of Christianity in the Western Church, was a central part of the liturgies of Holy Thursday where it reflected the merging of several different traditions and liturgies associated with Holy Thursday.[16] The contemporary Chrism Mass, now often celebrated in each diocese near the time of Holy Week if not on Holy Thursday itself, retains the centrality of this blessing of oils (for the sick, for the catechumens, and of the chrism) which are then brought back to parishes by their representatives present at the Mass and used as needed throughout the coming year.

In spite of this history of various practices, the addition in the contemporary rite of the option of the priest's blessing of the oil seems to undermine a long tradition of episcopal blessing of oil, thereby weakening the outward sign of the oil as tangible link to the larger Church through that annual Chrism Mass blessing. Certainly the presbyteral anointing of the oil still carries the juridical and imaginative tie to sacramental blessing and use, but a direct reference and understanding to the Church gathered around its bishop in worship and prayer is lost. What is gained, of course, is a necessary means for enacting the sacrament. The anointing of the sick often needs to be done in urgent and even emergency situations, presumably more so than the making of catechumens and other chrismations, and the lack of blessed oil (or lack of access to blessed oil) is addressed by this option of presbyteral blessing.

David Power, in his chapter on the anointing of the sick entitled "Open Questions," addresses a theological issue raised by this new option of presbyteral anointing in a way that gets to the heart of sacramental language. If the oil is already blessed, the priest is directed to make a prayer of thanksgiving over the oil, using the text as presented at PCS 123 (and again at PCS 140) which has a tripartite trinitarian structure, allowing for a brief anamnetic sentence under each section and concluding with a petition asking for the "God of mercy" to "ease the sufferings and comfort the weakness of" the ill person (PCS 123). The anamnetic/epicletic prayer of thanksgiving relies on a similar structure and, therefore, on a ritual meaning similar to the prayer of blessing, following the classic bipartite structure of anamnesis and epiclesis, and putting the emphasis, as expected, on the pneumatological epiclesis ("send the power of your Holy Spirit, the Consoler, into this precious oil, this soothing ointment, this rich gift, this fruit of the earth. Bless this oil + and sanctify it for our use" [PCS 123, second option]) rather than on the anamnetic bulk of the thanksgiving prayer. This comparison raised the question for Power whether the rite was presenting a blessing of something already blessed, and if so, what does it say about blessing in general, about the normativity and efficacy of the Chrism Mass event, and finally, about the relationship between episcopal and presbyteral ministry?

> Indeed, one may well ask whether the claim that this . . . [prayer of thanksgiving over the blessed oils] is not a blessing of oils already

blessed is not a conceptual fiction that derives from a consecratory and rather material notion of blessing, alien to the thought that it is within the blessing of God by the church that the blessing of people and things in God's name occurs. It is also a conceptual fiction that avoids the close epicletic conjunction between the invocation of the Spirit upon persons and things simultaneously, rather than separately. It is, however, a conceptual fiction that satisfies the more liturgically based desire to join anamnetic invocation of God with the actual anointing, without seeming to do violence to the more formal and juridical perception of episcopal powers and their effect.[17]

Thus, the pastoral solution to the very real situation of a lack of blessed oil in times of need raises a different set of issues, this time with sacramental and ecclesial concerns. Any good sacramental question should impact liturgies and rites other than the one in question, and this question is no exception in that it raises questions about the centrality and solemnity of the Chrism Mass vis-à-vis the lived experience of the anointing of the sick. How is the bishop a direct part of the anointing of the sick through his consecration of the oil in the Chrism Mass? Is it important, in light of a substantial history, that the bishop has a tangible sign of that relationship through the blessed oil? Can or should the blessed oil carry the weight of the ecclesial association of the sacrament? Is there a difference in efficacy between the anointing of the sick done with oil blessed at the Chrism Mass and the anointing of the sick done with oil blessed in the midst of the rite by the priest? Juridically, the answer to the final question must be *no,* as is clear in PCS 21 and as it is in any sacramental case where there is an ordinary situation ("The oil of the sick is ordinarily blessed by the bishop on Holy Thursday") and an extraordinary situation ("in case of necessity, any priest, but only within the celebration of the sacrament [may bless the oil of the sick]").[18] But the situating of the anointing of the sick within the larger spectrum of pastoral care of the sick has raised questions about how the sacrament of the anointing of the sick affects the other dimensions of pastoral care. An interesting situation was presented to this question by the Roman Catholic Church in Canada, which continued an optional "non-sacramental" rite of anointing with non-blessed oil, conceived of as a ritual to be used by family and friends of the sick person centered on a familiar element—oil—and the healing power of touch, along with appropriate prayers. How this anointing fits within the categories of sacramentality (sacrament, sacramental, non-sacramental), or how it is related to the sacrament of the anointing of the sick properly understood, proved difficult to define in many pastoral situations.[19] Because of its resemblance to the sacrament of the anointing of the sick, the ritual was ultimately considered to be confusing to the faithful and was dropped from newer ritual books.

A similar proposal, however, was made by John Huels at the Baltimore conference of May 2001[20] in which he challenged chaplains to consider the elements and rituals of Pastoral Care of the Sick that did not require a priest.[21] After reminding his audience of the ancillary sacramentals[22] and prayers of the *Book of Blessings,*[23] he turned to the question of the anointing with oil, suggesting a use of blessed oil (by a priest) that is neither the oil of the sick (the oil of the sacrament of anointing of the sick) nor unblessed oil:

> A very ancient practice in the Church, still observed today, is the application of blessed oil on sick persons. This is not the oil of the sick blessed by the bishop at the Chrism Mass for the sacrament of the anointing of the sick but is oil blessed by a priest or deacon using a distinct formula of blessing. The Roman Ritual contains a special blessing to be used as a sacramental for sick persons. Although this blessing is not taken up in the *Book of Blessings,* it may still be used as a pious practice or pious exercise.[24]

Absent from all the discussions of canon law and ritual efficacy is an image that is near and dear to the heart of the early Church, that of oil as the symbol of Christ,[25] the Anointed One. In baptism we put on Christ, becoming Christs and Christ's through the water and the anointing that incorporates us as priest, prophet and king. In each sacramental anointing the physical and spiritual remembrance of that christological anointing should call us to keep in mind our own baptism[26] and to see the anointing of the healing Christ as an ongoing participation in that baptismal anointing. This central symbol of Christ could help link a dominant theology in the first millennium of Christianity, that of oil itself as capable of carrying christological and ecclesial representation, to the different views of the second millennium. If approached in this way, the early Church variety of location and minister in the sacramental anointing of the sick might be easier to adopt and adapt in contemporary practices.

Finally, of the many theological issues raised by this trajectory of the "matter" of the sacrament of the anointing of the sick, a disturbing one is the fluctuating understanding of what constitutes "ecclesial" in the popular sense. Put simply, for many Christians, there seems to be a reduction of the idea of the Church to large gatherings where there is a sufficient number of people to physically and psychologically "fill their imagination." Especially for members of Generation X and younger, the visual images of concerts and the experience of large-group gatherings may be part of the influence. But the lived reality of this sacrament, the anointing of the sick, is that it often takes place in very small gatherings. Are we, as modern Christians, capable of imagining the reality of the Body of Christ in a domestic gathering, in a hospital room of only a few people, in and through an ordained minister (therefore appointed and official) of the Church?[27] How does the normative anointing of the sick, most frequently occurring in a hospital room with only the sick person and a priest present, embody an ecclesial sacrament in the popular mind? How do we overcome the disconnect for many younger Catholics between the ministry of the Church in all these situations and the popular cultural mindset in which large equals real? The anointing of the sick, like the sacrament of reconciliation, challenges the Church to re-articulate a popular understanding of Church as more than a critical mass of people gathered together, and which at the same time includes the intrinsic and extrinsic ecclesial value of the whole Body of Christ gathered together (here meaning the whole Body of Christ in a local, concrete manifestation with all the parts of the body, all the ranks, orders, and charisms represented).[28] Forty years after *Lumen Gentium*,[29] does "Church" still mean only the clergy, or only everyone all together? How do these popular conceptions (or misconceptions) affect our understanding of a sacramental rite that has two very different settings: individual and corporate (with a limitless number of options within those two settings)?

B. The Minister of the Rite

16. The priest is the only proper minister of the anointing of the sick.

    This office is ordinarily exercised by bishops, parish priests (pastors) and their assistants, chaplains of health care facilities, and superiors of clerical religious institutes.

17. These ministers have the pastoral responsibility both of preparing and helping the sick and others who are present, with

the assistance of religious and laity, and of celebrating the sacrament.

The diocesan bishop has the responsibility of supervising celebrations at which many sick persons may come together to receive the sacrament.

18. For a reasonable cause any other priest may confer this sacrament with at least the presumed consent of the minister mentioned in no. 16, whom the priest need only inform later.

19. When two or more priests are present for the anointing of a sick person, one of them may say the prayers and carry out the anointings, saying the sacramental form. The others may take the remaining parts, such as the introductory rites, readings, invocations, or instructions. Each priest may lay hands on the sick person.

The minister of the sacrament of the anointing of the sick, as described above, is not a separate issue from the matter and form discussion that preceded it or the two sections (on subject and efficacy) that follow. These questions are by their very nature intertwined, particularly when one reflects on ecclesiology and ministry in any sacramental rite.[30]

As with the discussion on oil and its implications above, there are two related arenas of discussion with regard to the meaning of the sacrament through the minister: one of a more pastoral nature, and in this case the more dominant discussion in American circles because of pastoral urgency, and another more theological, although again not unrelated to the pastoral.

Representation of the Proper Minister

When the priest anoints the sick, he is anointing in the name and with the power of Christ himself (see Mark 6:13). On behalf of the whole community, he is ministering to those members who are suffering (PCS 98).

Turning to the theological issues first, we find that, unlike the giving of Communion (including the "last Communion"—Viaticum), and unlike baptism in a number of situations, the anointing of the sick cannot be administered by a lay person or a deacon. Scholarship of recent decades has articulated two primary reasons, both theological and historical, for this restriction. The first has to do with the scripturally-informed "primary function" of the priest: that of his being a representative of the community.[31] While the sacrament is in the meeting between the action and wisdom of God, the faith of all present and the gathered Church acting and speaking with specific intent, the clarity of the ministerial restriction that the priest, as "proper" minister, represents the Church in a particular way leads us to see a representation beyond or different from that of the others named. On the one hand, this restriction is faithful to the foundational text of James, in which the command is to send for the "presbyters of the church" (Jas 5:14). On the other hand, the difficulty, as discussed above in Chapter One, is the interpretation (and even translation) of the word "presbyter"—who is, and who is not, a presbyter/elder? Closer in time to our own is the pivotal interpretation of the Council of Trent on this question, which, in countering the refutations of the Reformers, clarified for its constituency the equating of presbyter with priest, and that only the priest is the proper minister of this sacrament.

> If anyone says that the presbyters of the church who, as blessed James enjoins, should be brought in to anoint the sick person, are not priests who have been ordained by a bishop but the elders in any community; and that on that account the proper minister of last anointing is not exclusively a priest; *anathema sit*.[32]

John J. Ziegler has described the debates and ultimate decisions of the key Tridentine sessions concerned with extreme unction as revelatory of the tensions between those who saw the "current" form of the sacrament as correct and those who worried about the evidence to the contrary from earlier scriptural and ritual writings.[33] While the context of Vatican Council II was not the same as that of the Council of Trent,[34] the inheritance of the teaching as laid out in canon 4 of Trent remains in force, raising theological questions on the issue of representation—how and why does the priest represent the Church in a way that neither deacons nor baptized Christians serving as recognized ministers of the community do? Again, as with any fundamental sacramental question, this issue does not affect the anointing of the sick alone, but all the sacramental actions of the Church, and has been at the heart of much debate in recent decades. Whether it be the essential link between Eucharist and ordained priesthood, and therefore, by extension priesthood and all sacraments flowing from the Eucharist,[35] or the expansion outward from the Eucharist to embrace the wider sphere of ministry beyond ritual alone,[36] or the practical and pastoral reality of the need for a "public person" to lead a "public rite" and the theological understanding of how that public person is just that through appointment (ordination),[37] or any number of other articulate reflections on the key representation of the ordained presbyter,[38] the issue is central to our discussion on the anointing of the sick. The overarching discussion in recent writings has been the reinterpretation of Thomas Aquinas' articulation of the priest (particularly in the Eucharist) as standing *in persona Christi*, a theological perspective that has been stressed in recent Roman documents at the expense of (or the diminution of) the priest standing *in persona Ecclesiae*.[39] Each phrase has complex implications for the way sacraments work in the Church, but certainly a both/and rather than an either/or approach seems most faithful to Scripture and tradition:

> The ascending and pneumatological reading of *in persona Christi et Ecclesiae* renders the service theme of the presbyter and the leadership of the body clearly, in such a way as to emphasize the social reality of the priest's relation to the people and of his pastoral leadership within the community of the people.[40]

Such an approach, as carefully arrived at in Paul Philibert's clear and comprehensive article, allows for the maintenance of many of the key ideas recorded above: the source and fulfillment of anointing of the sick in the Eucharist, the conciliar concerns to broaden the ministerial imagination of priesthood into building up the Body of Christ in a variety of ways, the public person of the community linking the often individual encounter in anointing of the sick with the whole Church through the priest, and finally the relationality of human-divine encounters as the model for all sacramental ministry.

Anointing of the Sick and the Forgiveness of Sins

> If the sick person wishes to celebrate the sacrament of penance, it is preferable that the priest make himself available for this during a previous visit. If it is necessary to celebrate the sacrament of penance during the rite of anointing, it takes the place of the penitential rite (PCS 101).

The restriction of the anointing of the sick to an ordained presbyter has its roots in a second issue: the relationship between the anointing of the sick and reconciliation, or more directly, the relationship between anointing of the sick and the forgiveness of sins. This issue contributed to the shape of the sacrament as extreme unction at the time of the Council of Trent and continues to impact the proper minister of the sacrament today.

The historical restriction of the anointing of the sick to the ordained did not happen in a temporal moment, once and for all. Its gradual development was affected by the slow changes occurring in the sacrament of penance, from a system of public or canonical penance—harsh, demanding, and unique in a person's life—to a system of repeatable tariff penance.[41] Changes within the tariff penance system led to its systemization and regulations restricting the hearing of confessions, the assigning of penances, and the granting of absolution to priests. At the same time, cultural and ritual changes were leading the anointing of the sick away from a domestic ritual and from a ritual stressing physical healing to one that stressed spiritual healing. This spiritual healing could easily be seen as linked to the forgiveness of sins, especially when a Christian was overwhelmed with an illness that would most likely lead to death. The Jacobite *urtext* itself stressed the forgiveness of sins ("The prayer of faith will save the sick, and the Lord will raise them up; and anyone who has committed sins will be forgiven" [James 5:15]), and the move away both from the view of the human person as a psychosomatic whole and from the goal of physical healing, left this biblical legacy as one that has a stress on spiritual healing. It remained for a number of scholastic theologians to discuss and define how this forgiveness of sins differed from or complemented the other sacraments of forgiveness: baptism, Eucharist, and penance itself,[42] and for the canonization of that view at the Council of Trent.

The contemporary rite relies on a broader understanding and ritual observance of the forgiveness of sins through and adjacent to the anointing of the sick, particularly in the model of Christ, who "showed great concern for the bodily and spiritual welfare of the sick and commanded his followers to do likewise" (PCS 5). At the same time the rite notes that sickness is not to be "regarded as a punishment inflicted on each individual for personal sins" (PCS 2); it recognizes that sin and sickness, like emotional, mental, physical, and spiritual health, are mutually related and capable of affecting the whole human person ("Those who are seriously ill need the special help of God's grace in this time of anxiety, lest they be broken in spirit and, under the pressure of temptation, perhaps weakened in their faith" [PCS 5]). To effectively heal one part of the person is to address all the ills of that person, just as to be seriously sick is never solely a physical concern.

The relationship of this discussion to the minister, in this case a priest, may at first seem obtuse since the rite clearly suggests a preference for the sacrament of penance at a separate time (PCS 101), and it is that sacrament which has the primary link to presbyteral authority in the language of canon law and theology. The anointing of the sick, however, while speaking of the forgiveness of sins in a less juridical and more "medicinal" form of language[43] still recognizes the real forgiveness of sins when deemed "necessary":[44] "The healing of sin is not primary. Yet where sin complicates the process of healing, it too will be accounted for in God's promise."[45] In spite of this holistic view of healing and the more comprehensive formula in the contemporary rite,[46] the *praenotanda* still contributes to the sense of a reluctance to talk about physical healing ("A return to physical health *may* follow the reception of this sacrament if it will be beneficial to the sick person's salvation" [PCS 6]). In addition, the homiletic source of much reflection on the rite also avoids an emphasis on physical healing because of its apparent absence in many occasions of anointing.[47] This leads to a stress on other effects, most notably spiritual healing, and sharpens the distinction between sacramental healing and what might be termed the "trademark" of private (non-ecclesial) and charismatic (non-sacramental) healing—physical healing.[48]

These elements combine to reinforce the role of the priest as proper minister of the anointing of the sick both in the growing preference given to spiritual healing inclusive of the forgiveness of sins, in the unique representation of the priest as speaking in the name and power of Christ, and in the unique representation of the priest as standing for the Church in this sacrament.

In contemporary writings, counter arguments have been presented that address each level of the established tradition: biblical, historical tradition, and the theological issues of representation and forgiveness of sins. Those arguments can be summarized as follows. The controversy over the interpretation and translation of the key passage in James, already mentioned above in Chapter One, is that the definition of "elder" or "presbyter" did not mean sacerdotal priest (understood primarily as a cultic leader) at the time of writing, but rather representatives of the community. The checkered history of the sacrament of the anointing of the sick is not consistent nor compelling enough to limit the anointing to priests from the standpoint of tradition alone, but, to the contrary, actually supports anointing with blessed oil by other baptized Christians.[49] The issue of representation is less cut-and-dried, but the relationship between appointment by the community and official representation seems to be a key factor in recognizing others as "representative" of the ecclesial sacramental body. Deacons, by their ordination (appointment) and close connection ecclesially and pastorally to the ministry of the bishop, would be the most obvious representative, but baptized Christians, duly appointed and therefore ministering with the official status of the Church, could also be appropriate representatives. The complex and disputed issue of the priest standing *in persona Christi et Ecclesiae* in the Eucharist (and therefore in all the Church's sacraments) is probably the most important focus of theological discussion today because it is there that the deeper meaning of representation beyond deputizing is still being articulated.[50] In addition, the understanding of what it means to stand "in the person of Christ" has been a focus of theological reflection.[51] On the surface it would be foolish to deny that any baptized Christian does not stand in the person of Christ, having put on Christ in baptism and begun the lifelong journey towards formation in Christ through being Christ in the world, as well as having done this within the Body of Christ. But again, the theological ramifications of understanding the phrase *in persona Christi* as "linked to a descending theology" that "evokes God's call and the transforming power of the sacramental grace of holy orders,"[52] while at the same time discerning which is the prerequisite foundation, *in persona Christi* or *in persona Ecclesiae*,[53] are of a different order and are still the ground for profound theological disagreement about the sacramental, and thus ecclesial role, of the priest in sacramental actions.

The counterargument with regard to the historical and traditional link of anointing with the forgiveness of sins seems a bit easier to bridge. Baptized Christians (and even persons not baptized but with "the right intention") "may and sometimes must administer baptism . . . in imminent danger of death and especially at the moment of death, when no priest or deacon is available" (Christian Initiation, General Introduction, 16). Baptism forgives sins ("Baptism, the cleansing with water by the power of the living word, washes away every stain of sin, original and personal, and makes us sharers in God's own life and his adopted children," General Introduction of Initiation, 5), therefore this most fundamental of all sacraments which includes the forgiveness of sins, may, in extraordinary circumstances, be done by a lay person. The argument moves from this sacramental reality to the anointing of the sick, asking why in one case the laity may be entrusted with the administration of the sacrament but not in the other?[54] In addition, the rubrical separation of the sacrament of reconciliation from the sacrament of the anointing of the sick (PCS 101) would seem to support understanding the two sacraments as ritually separate, thereby opening the anointing of the sick to the ministration of extraordinary ministers when necessary.

These arguments for extending the faculties of the anointing of the sick, based on theological and historical reinterpretations, are not speculative in and by themselves. They are motivated, in part, by an urgent pastoral issue regarding the minister of the anointing of the sick, to which we now turn.

Pastoral Concerns Regarding the Proper Minister of Anointing of the Sick

The extension of the faculties for the anointing of the sick to allow for extraordinary ministers of the anointing, while still recognizing the ordinary minister as priest, has taken on an increasing urgency as the numbers of ordained priests available to anoint the sick has declined in the United States and beyond.[55] The gathering of the National Association of Catholic Chaplains in Baltimore in 2001 was an opportunity for the President of the NACC[56] to reflect on the make-up of the association's constituency.

> We NACC chaplains are many in number—nearly 3,400—and we are strong in our profession—70 percent board certified. We are women and men—70 percent and 30 percent, respectively. We are religious, lay, priests and deacons—48 percent, 32 percent, 17 percent, and 3 percent, respectively.

> As in so many other ministries of our post-Vatican II Church, women and men have responded to a baptismal call to pastoral care ministry. When our association was founded in 1965 at the threshold of our post-Vatican II Church, all the Catholic chaplains were ordained priests. Today only 17 percent are priests. Naturally this shift, like all significant change, brings both its strengths and its challenges.[57]

The statistics and numerical implications alone are able to reveal the pastoral concerns that have surfaced, but when they are joined to the stories and lived experiences of non-ordained hospital chaplains, family members of the sick and dying, and medical staff, then the overall picture of the decrease in availability of the sacrament becomes clear.[58] These anecdotal and statistical realities reflect the paradoxical nature of the current state of the sacrament of the anointing of the sick.

On the one hand, the fathers of the Second Vatican Council attempted to make the sacrament more available by renewing its meaning—identifying it truly as a sacrament for the seriously ill, not as a sacrament for the dying. On the other hand, as the number of priests continues to decline, the sacrament becomes less available for persons who are seriously ill.[59]

The success of the transition from popular understandings of extreme unction to sacrament for the sick has been a major source of many of the tensions within pastoral practice. The crisis of fewer hospital chaplains was first officially addressed in the United States in 1973 with a petition from the American Bishops' Committee on the Permanent Diaconate to the Sacred Congregation for the Sacraments and Divine Worship. In that petition, the committee asked for an extension of the faculties of anointing of the sick to include deacons.[60] The rejection of this petition was followed by further academic work and an additional proposal, authored by Fr. Paul Palmer, S.J., in 1975. The Bishops' Committee on the Permanent Diaconate also sponsored the petition, but this was rejected, and therefore the 1982 publication of *Pastoral Care of the Sick: Rites of Anointing and Viaticum* "upheld the present practice of the Church."[61] In 1994 the NACC itself sponsored a study, survey, and final white paper, asking for consideration of extension of faculties to deacons and certified hospital chaplains.[62] The 1997 Roman issuance of the *Instruction on Certain Questions Regarding the Collaboration of the Non Ordained Faithful in the Sacred Ministry of the Priest* answered by

> reaffirming the teaching that the priest and only the priest was the minister of the sacrament of the anointing of the sick. This clarification excluded any possibility of exploring an extension of the faculty to anoint beyond the current practice of the Church. The pastoral problem, however, did not cease nor did the questions and concerns.[63]

The pastoral problem is centered on the increasing acceptance of and desire for the sacrament of the sick at the same time as the actual availability of the sacrament has decreased. The NACC statistical study revealed that, while there was great variance between certain geographical areas in the USA and between rural and urban areas in particular, there is still a high percentage of hospitals that have to tell those requesting the sacrament that it is either unavailable altogether or unavailable for a period of time.[64] If the shortage of ordained priests in numerous areas prevents access to the anointing of the sick, many of the theological questions presented above, crucial or not, are moot, as they remain elements of theory, not of sacramental life. This shortage also raises questions about the non-sacramental elements (which form the majority) of the Pastoral Care of the Sick, which find their center, their "source and summit," in the anointing of the sick.

C. The Subject of the Anointing

8. The Letter of James states that the sick are to be anointed in order to raise them up and save them. Great care and concern should be taken to see that those of the faithful whose health is seriously impaired by sickness or old age receive this sacrament.

   Prudent or reasonably sure judgment, without scruple, is sufficient for deciding on the seriousness of an illness; if necessary a doctor may be consulted.

9. The sacrament may be repeated if the sick person recovers after being anointed and then again falls ill or if during the same illness the person's condition becomes more serious.

10. A sick person may be anointed before surgery whenever a serious illness is the reason for the surgery.

11. Elderly people may be anointed if they have become notably weakened even though no serious illness is present.

12. Sick children are to be anointed if they have sufficient use of reason to be strengthened by this sacrament. In case of doubt whether a child has reached the use of reason, the sacrament is to be conferred.

13. In public and private catechesis, the faithful should be educated to ask for the sacrament of anointing and, as soon as the right time comes, to receive it with full faith and devotion. They should not follow the wrongful practice of delaying the reception of the sacrament. All who care for the sick should be taught the meaning and purpose of the sacrament.

14. The sacrament of anointing is to be conferred on sick people who, although they have lost consciousness or the use of rea-

son, would, as Christian believers, have at least implicitly asked for it when they were in control of their faculties.

15. When a priest has been called to attend those who are already dead, he should not administer the sacrament of anointing. Instead, he should pray for them, asking that God forgive their sins and graciously receive them into the kingdom. But if the priest is doubtful whether the sick person is dead, he is to confer the sacrament, using the rite given in no. 269 [the emergency rite].

The anointing of the sick is not to be conferred on anyone who remains obdurately in open and serious sin.

In the post-conciliar years leading up to the promulgation of the new rite, the great concern in dealing with the recipient of anointing of the sick was encouraging people, through catechesis, to ask for the sacrament before the moment of death ("They should not follow the wrongful practice of delaying the reception of the sacrament"). This was in response to the prevailing tendency among many of the faithful to see extreme unction as only the final anointing, and the calling of the priest for the last rites only when there was no longer any hope for any recovery. As discussed above, the popular shift in understanding from an anointing of the dying to an anointing of the sick was not only fairly smooth but, in many places, enthusiastically embraced by active Roman Catholic parishioners, so much so that the opposite concern was also considered necessary to state in the general and specific introductions to the sacrament, namely that the anointing of the sick be sought only for serious illness, and not for every minor illness or injury.[65] Thus the first focus of the theological introductions regarding the subject or recipient of the anointing of the sick was who was the proper recipient, and how sick should they be? For the writers of the *praenotanda*, the difficulty in answering those questions is summarized in the extensive footnote explaining the translation of the Latin word *periculose*, by "seriously," rather than by "gravely," "dangerously," or "perilously."[66] Commentaries on the English translation of the Latin text have revealed a variety of positions by liturgical theologians and canon lawyers and point to just how difficult it is to define the parameters of what makes a person sufficiently sick but not necessarily dying, and therefore an appropriate recipient of anointing. Some popular understandings emerging from parish celebrations of the rite advocate its frequent celebration for virtually any illness or emotional upset, prompting concerned reactions against the practice.[67] More recent reflections on the definition of "how sick is sick enough" reveal the beginnings of a broad consensus on the issue. David Power sees in Italian interpretations of *periculose* a holistic understanding of the human person and a holistic healing rite.

> While the sacrament is for the physically ill, and may well have some physical effects, it is a celebration of faith and is intended for the spiritual strength of the sick, in face of their debility and danger. Hence . . . the proper criterion concerning apt subjects may not be in the physical order at all but in the spiritual. That is to say, the sacrament is for those who, being clinically ill, undergo serious spiritual crisis, making it difficult for them to sustain faith and hope, and to live human life with resolution and dignity.[68]

This same approach has been picked up by diverse contemporary commentators[69] who point to the need to view the healing as comprising not only physical wellbeing but also spiritual, physical, mental, and emotional healing as well.

> We should not perceive illness or old age as purely physical realities— they are much more. Christians pray for healing not only at a physical level but also at a psychological and spiritual depth that goes beyond what the eye can see. Celebrating the sacrament of the anointing of the sick in the presence of the community of family, friends, and neighbors awakens all present to the reality of limitation and frailty in our lives.[70]

This concern with an illness that potentially changes one's life, rather than with a temporary and minor inconvenience, has led to differences of opinion regarding whether chronic illnesses such as alcoholism and mental illness are legitimate reasons for anointing,[71] and whether old age itself warrants anointing without implying that it is of itself a serious illness.[72] In spite of those differences, chronic illnesses such as mental illnesses and severe alcoholism, long-term and frequently terminal illnesses such as AIDS and cancer, as well as debilitating diseases such as Alzheimer's, have generally come to be seen in pastoral circles as appropriate occasions for anointing, even repeated anointings, throughout the course of the illness.

In the study and preparation of the current rite these chronic illnesses have, as mentioned, raised the issue of whether the anointing of the sick could be repeated. The Tridentine conclusions reflect the scholastic sense that extreme unction was the final anointing, and therefore done only once, and if the sick person did recover, the reception of anointing carried with it ongoing obligations. To accept the anointing was to accept the consequences.[73] PCS 9 suggests several scenarios in which the anointing may be done more than once, either because of recovery and then relapse, or changes within the course of the same illness. This is reiterated in PCS 102, where the articulation regarding repeated anointing is expanded: "the sacrament of anointing may be repeated when in the pastoral judgment of the priest the condition of the sick person warrants the repetition of the sacrament." Interpreting these paragraphs through other sections of the general instruction would imply that the relapse or prolongation of illness may very well result in a loss of hope or faith that would be restored by the repeated anointing ("Those who are seriously ill need the special help of God's grace in this time of anxiety, lest they be broken in spirit and, under the pressure of temptation, perhaps weakened in their faith" [PCS 5]).

The Anointing of the Sick and the Theology of Participation

Underlying a number of the instructions in this section on "Recipients of the Anointing of the Sick" is the presumption of the participation of the sick person him- or herself themselves in the rite. In spite of the subtitle "recipient," which could imply a passivity on the part of the person to be anointed, the introduction to the rite calls for an active and distinct role for the sick person. This is evident particularly in the extraordinary instruction (in the case of the recipient being unconscious), when anointing is to be administered only if the person "would . . . have at least implicitly *asked* for it when they were in control of their faculties" [PCS 14].[74] The assumption is that the sick person will be able to articulate when they feel the fear, loss of hope, temptation, or despair that can often accompany serious illness, and "ask for the sacrament of anointing, as soon as the right time comes" [PCS 13]. If they are not able to discern and physically request it for themselves, someone who knows their spiritual life is to speak for them, as implied in PCS 14.

The point of this participation, perhaps outwardly exemplified in the personal request for the sacrament but certainly not summarized therein, is the same active engagement in sacramental encounter that underlies all of the sacraments. The general introduction is clear that, as with all sacraments, active participation in its most profound theological sense is necessary here also.

> In the anointing of the sick, which includes the prayer of faith, faith itself is manifested. *Above all this faith must be made actual both in the minister of the sacrament and, even more importantly, in the recipient.* The sick person will be saved by personal faith and the faith of the Church, which looks back to the death and resurrection of Christ, the source of the sacrament's power, and looks ahead to the future kingdom that is pledged in the sacraments.[75]

Participation here does not mean, of course, the external liturgical participation of responding to prayers, singing all the songs, and reciting all the required texts, even though that is important and often the interpretation of the key passage in the Constitution on the Sacred Liturgy.[76] Rather, theological participation begins with the *perichoresis* of the divine Trinity into which the baptized Christian is drawn through the water bath, anointing, and eucharistic Communion, participating through participation in Christ in the economy of God. This theological articulation of participation is the response of duty and delight to the gift of faith, and the foundation on which all ritual, ethical, and sacramental participation is built. Anointing of the sick is a sacrament of faith in which faith will be made manifest, not because of some magical alignment of words, gestures, and oil, but because of the power of Christ and the prayer made in his name, the faith of the minister, the faith of the recipient, and the faith of the Church. This theological line of thinking is the reason for the ancient restriction that only the baptized in communion with the Church could receive the anointing with blessed oil (as was also the case for the one doing the anointing),[77] and for the contemporary restriction that the anointing "is not to be conferred on anyone who remains obdurately in open and serious sin" (PCS 15).

In a paradoxical way, so present in much of Christian experience, the sick are more actively participatory here than in some other sacramental encounters, again not because they engage in the ritual to a greater degree, but because they participate through their baptism *and* through their suffering in Christ. The anointing of the sick recalls the baptismal anointing by which each Christian became *christos* and then joins that reality to the reality of the sick person, allowing "the suffering and separation of sickness to become identified as participation in the *pascha Christi*. By such anointing, *anamnesis* is made of the passage of Christ through death to life and of the patient's consecration to this mystery."[78] This participation in the suffering of Christ is not a desire to suffer, which is unhealthy in any circumstance, but the way in which the sick Christian is confirmed in understanding that sickness and suffering do exist and do have meaning ("From Christ's words [the sick] know that sickness has meaning and value for their own salvation, and for the salvation of the world" [PCS 1]). The introduction to the rite is clear in stressing that the sick person must fight against illness (as should all who surround and assist the sick [PCS 3, 4]); however, "we should always be prepared to fill up what is lacking in Christ's sufferings for the salvation of the world as we look forward to creation's being set free in the glory of the children of God" (PCS 3). This is neither the struggle of a lone individual, nor of an individual alone with their God, because it is, as with all the sacraments, a sacrament of the Church. The communion in anointing is of all the manifestations of the "body." "When we anoint the body of a sick person, we anoint not only that individual but also the ecclesial body of Christ."[79] The body of Christ that is the Church is thus sacramentally bound to the suffering of the sick individual through, with, and in Christ in the anointing of the sick.

The Ministry of the Sick

This participation in the paschal mystery is part of the ministry of the sick to the Church and to the world. As mentioned above, too often the sick are considered passive recipients of our prayers and ministrations, without thought given to their role as minister to all those with whom they come in contact. The General Introduction describes their role as one of a "reminder":

> Moreover, the role of the sick in the Church is to be a reminder to others of the essential or higher things. By their witness the sick show that our mortal life must be redeemed through the mystery of Christ's death and resurrection. (PCS 3)

This ministry of witness to "essential things" is, again, not simply through the passivity of being sick in our midst, but through challenging us to be compassionate and to engage in acts of prayer and mercy. This calls us to be the hands and feet of Christ for others, which is ultimately a good; however, there is more than that at issue. "The sick are understood to have access to an existential grasp of the paschal mystery, and so a measure of divine wisdom unavailable elsewhere in the Church."[80] Their experience of being seriously sick reminds us of our own immortality and turns our thoughts from the mundane events of daily life, giving us an insight into the paschal mystery, and reminding us that this is a mystery not just of the efficacious death and resurrection of Christ, but of our own engagement into that passage of life and death also. Their "existential grasp" "discovers God in a particular way and reveals this to the community,"[81] and in that revelation we become "agents with them of the world's salvation."[82]

This revelation embodies two key aspects of contemporary sacramental theology that are particularly central in the anointing of the sick. The first is that sacramentality is never generic; sacraments are always specific in time and place, as well as mediated through and engaged in material and temporal reality.[83] In the anointing of the sick this specificity is manifest in the variety of circumstances and ritual adaptations necessary to the unique encounter that each anointing is between the sick person, the Church and God, and in the corporeal reality of sickness and suffering which is the means of revelation of the paschal mystery. "A sacrament has both its reality and its meaning only in a concrete existential happening."[84]

The second theological concept is captured in the biblical and historical interpretation of healing as a sign of the reign of God. As healing overcomes death and reveals the promise of immortality, and the oil (particularly perfumed oil) is symbolic of the "oil of paradise,"[85] so the sick person witnesses to our future fulfillment in concrete and specific ways. This eschatological dimension of anointing stands in a necessary and positive tension with the anamnetic dimensions of healing rites based on the historical actions of Jesus and their development in the Church's tradition. In relation to this eschatological role, the rite must not "be limited to consoling words and strengthening gestures" but it must also proclaim this "liberation" of a new vocation and new future, as well as the reality of the suffering Christ and the suffering Christian in Christ.[86]

This prophetic role of the sick person in our midst, through their conforming to the "Anointed One,"[87] transforms "the community's consciousness through the witness of [the sick person's] own confrontation with mortality."[88]

> By his own anointing, then, the sick person is identified with Jesus Christ in his suffering and death, under the promise made to him and through him to the community, that the one who suffers in the Lord may, even in the midst of his suffering, trust in the resurrection. Death shall be, but it shall not be the end.[89]

D. The Effects of the Sacrament

5. Those who are seriously ill need the special help of God's grace in this time of anxiety, lest they be broken in spirit and, under the pressure of temptation, perhaps weakened in their faith.

    This is why, through the sacrament of anointing, Christ strengthens the faithful who are afflicted by illness, providing them with the strongest means of support.

    The celebration of this sacrament consists especially in the laying on of hands by the priests of the Church, the offering of the prayer of faith, and the anointing of the sick with oil made holy by God's blessing. This signifies the grace of the sacrament and confers it.

6. This sacrament gives the grace of the Holy Spirit to those who are sick: by this grace the whole person is helped and saved, sustained by trust in God, and strengthened against the temptations of the Evil One and against anxiety over death. Thus the sick person is able not only to bear suffering bravely, but also fight against it. A return to physical health may follow the reception of this sacrament if it will be beneficial to the sick person's salvation. If necessary, the sacrament also provides the sick person with the forgiveness of sins and the completion of Christian penance.

25. Through this holy anointing
    may the Lord in his love and mercy help you
    with the grace of the Holy Spirit.

    May the Lord who frees you from sin
    save you and raise you up.

98. In the course of his visits to the sick, the priest should try to explain two complementary aspects of this sacrament: through the sacrament of anointing the Church supports the sick in their struggle against illness and continues Christ's messianic work of healing. All who are united in the bond of a common baptism and a common faith are joined together in the body of

Christ since what happens to one member affects all. The sacrament of anointing effectively expresses the share that each one has in the sufferings of others. When the priest anoints the sick, he is anointing in the name and with the power of Christ himself. On behalf of the whole community, he is ministering to those members who are suffering. This message of hope and comfort is also needed by those who care for the sick, especially those who are closely bound in love to them.

107. The Church's use of oil for healing is closely related to its remedial use in soothing and comforting the sick and in restoring the tired and the weak. Thus the sick person is strengthened to fight against the physically and spiritually debilitating effects of illness. The prayer for blessing the oil of the sick reminds us, furthermore, that the oil of anointing is the sacramental sign of the presence, power, and grace of the Holy Spirit.

It should be apparent from the numbering of the paragraphs above that the introductions to the effects of the sacrament—unlike those for the issues of matter and form, the minister, and the subject—are scattered throughout both the General Introduction and the Introduction to the Anointing of the Sick proper. The fact that the effects of the sacrament are not found in a discreet category parallels what David Power has pointed out, that the effects are not another neatly defined category by which we can understand a facet of the sacrament of anointing, but rather the source of the other three categories that flow out of sacramental effect.[90] In other words, to ask what the sacrament does will influence who receives it, who administers it, and how they do it.

The classic language of sacramental efficacy in which the sacrament is said to signify what it effects ("signifies the grace of the sacrament and confers it" [PCS 5]), is presented in the anointing of the sick with reference to the three primary actions discussed in the previous chapter. But by reviewing all the "effects" summarized or alluded to in the paragraphs presented above, the reader is reminded both that sacraments, as symbols, are polyvalent, and that the broad spectrum of their effects forms a rich multiplicity of meanings. One way of approaching the effects of this sacrament is to ask what it does with regard to healing, and what is healed.

In our modern or postmodern worldview the answer to what should be healed is probably the most literal and concrete response to an obvious answer—the body. After all, what else is there? One of the great challenges of sacramental theology and language is that there is always more to sacraments than meets the eye, more than can be perceived by human senses, or at least that human senses are the first level portals to worlds only imagined and "sensed" in other ways. In a world of impoverished literalism, of post-symbolic, post-metaphorical interests, sacramental reality is a hard sell. From this perspective, if the body is not healed, the sacrament did not work. And from a theological perspective, if the sacrament did not work, if the body was not obviously healed, then it may demonstrate the "non-appearance" or absence of God, either because God is not God, or, perhaps worse, that God chooses not to heal but to punish—the "God of the ambush" in Charles Gusmer's terms.[91] But sacramental grace is always offered and present,[92] which returns us to the realm of sacramental theology and Christian anthropology.

One approach to understanding how the sacrament is efficacious is to begin with the distinction between curing and healing. To use medical language, which will be explored further in the next chapter, the process of curing isolates a particular injury or illness and treats the symptoms, through the agency of a specialist trained to deal with the specific problem. Healing, in the sacramental sense, may incorporate cure, but it is a much broader category, focused on holistic integration and restoration of relationships, both internal and external. The theological paragraphs of the introductions use the words "strengthen," "sustain," "trust," and "support," as descriptors of healing. Gusmer interprets these as ways the rite responds to and overcomes different levels of alienation. The first alienation is a breakdown in wholeness within an individual, where not only does one's body not do what one wills it to do, but the primary vehicle of human expression—the body—seems to turn against the individual and express something very different than what the person hopes to be presenting or communicating to the world. The second is the breakdown in communal wholeness, exemplified by breaks with one's environment, family, routine, and Church. The rite also addresses the third breakdown in relationship, the relationship with God, which can result in confrontation and distance, or anger and rejection at a God who seems to be absent, or a focus on self-recrimination that requires asking "what did I do wrong to deserve this?"[93] These three levels or dimensions of alienation—with one's self, with the multiple communities that each of us belongs to, and with God—have been addressed by other theologians in similar ways, most notably by David Power and Jennifer Glen.[94] The recurring presence of these alienations in studies on the anointing of the sick points to the centrality of this idea of healing as a return to wholeness on different levels and its association with salvation. Salvation is a union with the divine, and therefore this unity of person, community, and human-divine relationship becomes one of the primary manifestations of the eschatological dimension in the anointing of the sick.

Keeping in mind the breadth of healing and the distinction between cure and healing, one of the critiques of the present rite has been its reticence to ask for physical healing. PCS 6 states that "a return to physical health may follow the reception of this sacrament if it will be beneficial to the sick person's salvation."

> Sick persons who are the subject of this ecclesial action could be forgiven for desiring greater boldness on the part of the praying church. They might well wish the church to speak with the audacity of the psalmist calling for complete restoration of health . . . The church has precedence for greater boldness regarding physical healing in its prayer texts if it considers one of its sourcebooks, the prayers of the prophets and psalmist and of those who approached Jesus . . . "Sir, if you want to you can cure me" (Matt 8.3). Reticence about praying for physical healing as an outcome of bodily anointing was certainly understandable in the centuries when physical anointing was delayed until the deathbed, and was truly extreme unction. The reticence is less understandable when the church surrounds with prayer, love, trust and faith those struggling believers whose health is seriously impaired . . . New subjects for this Rite of Anointing—seriously ill believers rather than dying ones—invite new attitudes in prayer. The *Ordo* is conventional rather than prophetic in this regard.[95]

A contributing cause of the mentality Mary Collins critiques above is the persistence of the mind/body dichotomy in Western theology. This persistence runs so deep that what may be subconsciously under consideration is the idea that physical healing is not important and certainly not the realm in which the all powerful God would consider getting involved. This perception can lead to prayer considered more appropriate: for what is more like God, spiritual healing and prayer for the things of above, or physical healing? The great irony of this misunderstanding, of course, is that these prayers for healing are in the midst of sacramental action, dependent on physical touch and the very physical material of oil. In addition, contemporary Christian anthropology views the human person as a psychosomatic whole in which the understanding of the interrelatedness of the person is not only closer to the world of the New Testament writings and the early Church, but is also more consistent with movements in the world of contemporary medicine.

This psychosomatic whole is the anthropological presumption underlying the issue of healing the whole person—physically, emotionally, and spiritually—that must, therefore, include the healing of sin. One of the most difficult issues for many seriously ill Christians (and for the "co-suffering" families and friends[96]) is the sense that this illness is somehow "deserved" or is at least divine punishment for personal transgressions long forgotten and confessed. Even among faithful Christians, whose own beliefs as well as catechetical training tell them otherwise, the question most often addressed to hospital chaplains is related to "what did I do" and "how can I undo it?"[97] The contemporary rite tries to address the theoretical connection between sickness and sin by first stating that, "although closely linked with the human condition, sickness cannot as a general rule be regarded as a punishment inflicted on each individual for personal sins" (PCS 2). While the passive voice of this sentence may lead the reader to hear it in an ambiguous way, its location in the beginning section of the Introduction is a clear rejection of the type of claims made by some Christian groups that widespread epidemics such as AIDS are divine punishment for personal actions. The Church is also placing itself at a particular point on the spectrum of Christian thought on the issue of sickness and sin. In other words, the theological introduction to the rite and the rite itself are not saying that there is *no* relationship between sin and sickness—a perspective that also seems to be in vogue in some Christian circles—but they are rejecting an image of a vengeful God exacting a toll through human suffering and sickness.

So how is the rite inviting us to understand the relationship between sin and sickness and what has that to do with the effects of the sacrament? The key, of course, is that one of the effects of the anointing of the sick is the forgiveness of sin. "If necessary, the sacrament also provides the sick person with the forgiveness of sins and the completion of Christian penance" (PCS 6). Because it would be hard to imagine any one of us not in need of forgiveness, one can assume that the forgiveness of sins is part of every anointing. Two primary theological points emerge from this reality. The first is the view of the human person as the psychosomatic whole described above. The Church and many Western cultures have learned from the social sciences, hard sciences, and other cultures[98] that the human person is interrelated internally. If one is suffering emotionally, the physical body will be affected. If there is a profound spiritual crisis, the emotional, and mental, and perhaps physical dimensions of the individual will be affected, and so on. This means that to "treat" one dimension of the person the whole person needs to be examined and engaged. Far different than the technical cure, which isolates and treats a single problem, healing requires all the dimensions of the person to be addressed. This *cura personalis* is not a new idea in the Church, but rather an ancient understanding represented and rediscovered.[99] This spiritual healing metaphor also had a strong trajectory in reconciliation rites in the Eastern Church.[100] Therefore, to effect healing through the sacrament of anointing is to address whatever ills are tearing at the fabric of human wholeness, including but not limited to the spiritual illness of sin. This holistic healing is to counter the alienations as described by Gusmer, and to give the sick person (and all those gathered around that individual) the strength to overcome brokenness. A Flemish description summarizes this healing in a wonderfully succinct way by describing the effects of the anointing of the sick as being "healed to life," with all that that entails.[101]

A second theological focus regarding sin and sickness is related to the economy of God and our perception of the divine purposes of sickness. The contemporary over-reaction against any association of sin and sickness is understandable in light of the sometime historical understanding that the forgiveness of sins was the only effect of the anointing of the sick. But to divorce sin from sickness completely, or to say that there is no theological meaning in sickness, is to secularize it completely.[102] "Human sickness derives from our sinful alienation, healing is a divine reality that aims at our wholeness before God."[103] The concrete danger of rejecting any relation of sin and sickness, and even the relationship between personal sin and sickness (not as cause and effect but as relational reality), is that it can lead to the conclusion that if the sickness is not in any way related to our sin, it must be the will of a wrathful God. The logical response to that, for those concerned to image God in different ways, is that our merciful God always desires health. Anything else is not the will of God and therefore has no positive meaning. The pitfalls of that trajectory should be apparent, particularly in the two inevitable next steps. If a sick individual does not return to health, he or she is somehow thwarting God's will or invoking a particular wrath. In addition, the assumption that only good health is in the economy of God is to deny any meaning to sickness and suffering—theologically, sacramentally, or personally. "To say that it is God's will that all be in good health is to skirt the paschal mystery,"[104] the premise on which the whole rite and its *praenotanda* are based. The very title of the opening paragraph, "Human Sickness and its Meaning in the Mystery of Salvation" states clearly that sickness does have meaning, and that God's wisdom for each individual Christian may be beyond human comprehension.

> Suffering and illness have always been among the greatest problems that trouble the human spirit. Christians feel and experience pain as do all other people; yet their faith helps them to grasp more deeply the mystery of suffering and to bear their pain with greater courage. From Christ's words they know that sickness has meaning and value for their own salvation and for the salvation of the world (PCS 1).

Within this context, a primary effect of the sacrament is revealed as the tension (the life-giving tension) between struggling to regain health ("part of the plan laid out by God's providence is that we should fight strenuously against all sickness and carefully seek the blessings of good health, so that we may fulfill our role in human society and in the Church" [PCS 3]), and accepting, when appropriate, a different definition of health and healing.[105] In some cases, the effect may be complete health, at other times it may be a healing that moves to a different horizon of future possibilities.

Thus far the discussion on the effects of the sacrament has dealt with aspects that are particular to the anointing of the sick or held in common among a few sacraments. But with all the sacramental actions of the Church, there are those effects, signified through the rite and explicated in the theological introduction, which are common to all. The most prominent is the communication of "grace," described in several different ways. If grace is fundamentally the self-communication of God, it raises the question, what exactly of God is being communicated? The answer is *presence,* the presence of God. Classic Christian theology, particularly Eastern Christian theology, is clear that sacraments do not make God present, God is always present, even if in varying ways, and there is nothing that humans can do to manipulate God into doing what God does not will (hence the difference between sacrament and magic). If the primary healing of the anointing of the sick is the overcoming of alienation, at all levels, then the breaching of the gap between the sick individual and God is this grace, this revelation of Godself. This does not happen through a supernatural appearing, but rather through the divine gift of human discernment, in our ability to see and know the presence of God in our midst, primarily through other human beings and the ministry of those human beings in the Church.[106] So, part of the grace of each sacrament is the strength, the comfort, and the help in knowing in a particular way the presence of God in this post-incarnation time. As Christ revealed God in the world in a more profound way, the sacraments now reveal that presence analogously, not denying the omnipresence of God, but showing a particular presence of God through the actions of the Church.[107] Contemporary Western theology develops that idea as the integral relationship between creation and sacramentality. The same creating God is the source and object of this grace in the sacrament, but God is present differently in the sacramental event as opposed to creation. The key to the difference is that "sacraments involve created human beings responding to their already creating God in an act of appropriation."[108] This response, what the theological introduction calls "faith" ("The sick person will be saved by personal faith and the faith of the Church" [PCS 7]), grounds the discernment of the grace of the sacrament.

Discerning the face of God is not, however, an individual activity, especially in relation to sacraments in general and to the anointing of the sick in particular. First, the role of the community is necessary as a check against misinterpreting the self-communication of God ("self-delusion points to the need for community").[109] Second, the community is the recipient of the insight and discernment the sick individual gains by participation in this sacrament, and which increases the individual's faith and through it a deeper participation in the paschal mystery. Having received grace, the anointed one images a "relationship with a dimension of transcendence."[110] Thus, in the anointing of the sick, "the accent is not on healing, not on forgiving, nor on preparing for death. It is on the sick person, who through this experience discovers God in a particular way and reveals this to the community. All other factors enter in, but they are related to this as organizing center."[111]

The contemporary rite has restored in text and action (and theological introduction) the fullness of this presence as that of the Triune God. Absent in the ritual language of earlier rites was the prominent inclusion of the Holy Spirit, an absence now remedied. "This sacrament gives the grace of the Holy Spirit to those who are sick: by this grace the whole person is helped and saved, sustained by trust in God, and strengthened against the temptations of the Evil One and against anxiety over death" (PCS 6). The epicletic dimensions of the rite reveal the trinitarian scope of this self-communication; in the laying on of hands, in the prayer of blessing of oil, and in the anointing formula itself. When coupled with the strongly christological emphasis on the scriptural roots and model of Jesus' own healing, and surrounded by the address of most of the prayer texts to the First Person of the Trinity who jointly sends the Holy Spirit and grants help in "his love and mercy," the fullness of the understanding of trinitarian involvement is revealed.[112]

This move away from a solely christological/anamnetic focus to a pneumatological/epicletic focus grounded in trinitarian theology restores the anointing of the sick to the eschatological integrity of its scriptural basis. In the Gospels, the healing actions of Jesus are both about compassion for an individual or group of individuals and about revealing the kingdom of God here and now. In a similar way, the Church continues the ministry of Jesus both by drawing on that historical and timeless power "of the name" and by witnessing to the reign of God in our midst. The anointed individual is not restored to a previous state, but, as in any rite of passage, moves to a new place, "essentially connected with the future: [the anointing] includes arriving at a new harmony, a new integration of one's situation, and a new outlook, operative at every level on which the sick person has been affected by illness."[113] One would presume, from a normative cultural perspective, that sickness would not be an opportunity for new life, let alone hope for the future. However, hope for tomorrow is the primary context of meaning.

> Expectation is essential to meaning. The expected future is the horizon within which we judge and interact with the present . . . When the expected future is snatched away and replaced with some totally alien alternative, the present loses its meaning for me, until I can reconstruct a projected future with which to act.[114]

Not only does serious sickness demand that the projected future be reconstructed, but "the vision of death lurking within the experience of sickness seems to cut off the future absolutely, at least from the experiential and imaginative viewpoint,"[115] resulting in the potential loss of hope for any imagined future. This is where the sacramental efficacy of the anointing comes in, because it can say to the sick person "in sure and confident hope" that there is a future. From the perspective of faith, the healing not only leads to a "new vocation" for the individual but also to new revelations for all those who care for and engage with the anointed individual. Consequently, whether a cure occurs or not, a hope is made concrete because of the manifestation of the reign of God and the mercy of God in and through this individual who then witnesses to the larger Christian community and to the world. This reversal of our common assumptions prevents sickness from remaining a trap, an "enclosure" with no future when speaking of serious and often terminal illness. It can become instead a threshold, a liminal space, in which the God of creation and of sacrament works and invites the individual, and all who journey with and through that individual, out of multiple alienations and into new depths of connections within oneself, within communities, and with God.

These various manifestations of healing both point to the ritual expression of what is unique in the sacrament of the anointing of the sick and what unites it to all other sacramental action. Sacramental efficacy is multivalent enough to invite a greater degree of theological reflection than perhaps the other three classic issues, but is less of a magnet for pastoral controversy than is currently found in the arenas of minister and subject. Sacraments always work, and no "sacrament is intended simply to confer grace on an individual."[116] These two realities allow the issue of efficacy to be a rich source for sacramental theology both in the specificity of anointing of the sick and in the broader realm of all sacramental action.

Conclusion

The four classic sacramental issues presented here: matter and form, minister, subject, and sacramental effects, are not solely historical issues, important only in those discussions and times when the contemporary rite was being formed from tradition and pastoral experience following the mandates of Vatican II. Instead, they continue to form and inform consensus and differences among new generations of theologians concerned with the theological integrity of the anointing of the sick as well as its pastoral reality, experience, and effectiveness. These four categories, which open up into the possibility of so many more sub-categories, are not exhaustive. Particularly in the last decade, a number of other issues, often arising out of dialogue between theology, ritual practice, and issues important in the larger world, have resulted in new questions and new connections. These issues, some well-discussed and well-formed, others too new to be thoroughly analyzed, form the basis of the next chapter.

They point to the reality that the anointing of the sick is a living, organic reality, always being reformed in order to both express and embody faith.

Notes, Chapter Three

[1] "The Sacrament of Anointing: Open Questions" *The Pastoral Care of the Sick,* ed. Mary Collins and David N. Power (London: SCM Press, 1991) 95–107.

[2] Sickness and Symbol: The Promise of the Future," *Worship* 54 (1981) 397–411.

[3] John J. Ziegler, *Let Them Anoint the Sick* (Collegeville: Liturgical Press, 1987).

[4] *Disputed Questions in the Liturgy Today* (Chicago: LTP, 1988) 91–99.

[5] The May 2001 gathering in Baltimore resulted in a publication of the major presentations under the title *Recovering the Riches of Anointing: A Study of the Sacrament of the Sick,* ed. Genevieve Glen (Collegeville: Liturgical Press, 2002).

[6] And whether the oil itself is "the sacrament" . . . "The question here is whether blessed oil is itself a sacrament to be administered or whether the act of anointing is the sacrament" (Susan K. Wood, "The Paschal Mystery: The Intersection of Ecclesiology and Sacramental Theology in the Care of the Sick," *Recovering the Riches of Anointing,* 17).

[7] This was, however, not the only tradition, and seems to have been more central in reality and in theological imagery in the first eight hundred years of Christianity than in the Middle Ages. Consistent with the reforms of Vatican II, it is those earlier centuries that provide the favored historical context and theology for liturgical reforms.

[8] The classic early text describing this is the letter of Pope Innocent I to Decentius of Gubbio in 416, cited in Robert Cabié, "La letter du Pape Innocent Ier à Décentius de Gubbio," *Bibiothèque de la Revue d'Histoire Ecclésiastique* 58 (Louvain, 1974): "Quod non est dubium de fidelibus aegrotantibus accipi vel intelligi debere qui sancto oleo chrismatis perungui possunt quod (oleum) ab eposcopo confectum, non solum sacerdotibus sed et omnibus uti christianis licet, in sua aut in suorum necessitate unguendum."

[9] Power, "Open Questions," 96. It should be noted that the historical evidence does not support an unbroken tradition of the bishop blessing the oil, particularly the sacramentary traditions which reveal a variety of approaches between the eighth and the tenth centuries.

[10] See Peter Brown, *The Cult of Saints: Its Rise and Function in Latin Christianity* (Chicago: University of Chicago, 1981) 1.

[11] For a good overview of the tradition and the relationship between archeological and liturgical evidence, see I. H. Dalmais, "Memoire et vénération des Saints dans les églises de traditions syriennes," *Saints et sainteté dans la liturgie,* ed. A. Tri- acca and A. Pistoia (Rome: CLV Edizione Liturgiche, 1987).

[12] For a different opinion on the categorization of this practice, see Ann Ball, *A Handbook of Catholic Sacramentals* (Huntington, IN: Our Sunday Visitor Pub. Division, 1991) 194–95. She prefers to draw a defining boundary between what could be considered the sacrament of anointing of the sick and a sacramental more in line with popular piety surrounding the practices of the official liturgy.

[13] Brown, *The Cult of Saints,* especially chs. 4 and 6.

[14] Cited in Lizette Larson-Miller, "Women and the Anointing of the Sick," *Coptic Church Review* 12 (1991) 44–45. For the fuller version of the story, see "Life of St. Geneviève," cited in Antoine Chavasse, *Etude sur l'onction des infirmes dans l'église latine du iii au xi siècle.* Vol. I, *Du iii siècle au la réforme carolingienne* (Lyon: En depot, Librairie du Sacré-Coeur, 1942).

[15] The earliest texts of pontifical liturgies from Rome clearly have the pope or another bishop consecrating the chrism, but the oil of the catechumens (exorcistic) and the oil for the sick are not as clear. See Antoine Chavasse, *Le Sacramentaire Gélasien* (*Vaticanus Reginensis* 316*)* (Tournai: Desclée, 1958); Joseph Jungmann, *Mass of the Roman Rite,* trans. Francis A. Brunner, Rev. Charles K. Riepe (Westminster, MD: Christian Classics, 1980) 455; and Cyrille Vogel, *Medieval Liturgy: An Introduction to the Sources,* trans. William Storey and Niels Rasmussen (Washington, D.C.: The Pastoral Press, 1986). Evidence from the oldest texts of the Gelasian sacramentaries reveal a "primitive benediction of the oil of the sick and the catechumens" (Chavasse, p. 133) but these are not necessarily liturgies presided over by a bishop. It appears that the priests of the titular churches may have presided at these liturgies, and consequently have been the presiders doing the consecration of the oils (Chavasse, p. 139). Further complicating this is the evidence from the *Hadrianum* that, unlike the chrism and the exorcistic oil which were prepared "in house" by the clergy, the oil of the sick was both brought to the liturgy by the faithful and was "blessed at the demand of the faithful" (Chavasse, p. 139). The *ordines* of the eighth century also represent the Roman (?) tradition that the Pope alone blessed the chrism, and possibly the other oils, but "did not reserve these to himself," supporting the evidence from the Gelasian sacramentary traditions (Chavasse, p. 128). Finally, the Romano-Germanic pontificals of the tenth century show the benediction of all the oils reserved to the bishop, but the blessing of the chrism is situated in a more central position in the canon, whereas the blessing of the oil of the sick comes in the concluding doxology, revealing this mixed history in the liturgical books (Jungmann, p. 261).

[16] See the discussion in Gerard Austin, *The Rites of Confirmation: Anointing with the Spirit* (New York: Pueblo, 1985) 102–12; Matthew J. O'Connell, "Reflections on the Mass and Blessing of Chrism," *Liturgy for the People: Essays in Honor of Gerald Ellard* (Milwaukee: Bruce Pub. Co., 1963) 55–74; and Kenneth Stevenson, *The Liturgical Meaning of Holy Week: Jerusalem Revisited* (Washington, D.C.: The Pastoral Press, 1988) 41–44.

[17] Power, "Open Questions," 97.

[18] Here, the most common example (or best known to many people) is the reception of communion from either the "ordinary" minister of communion (priest, deacon) or from an "extraordinary" minister of communion (usually here, a lay person). In spite of some popular opinion, the body and blood of Christ are not somehow "holier" because they are given by clergy as opposed to laity.

[19] *Pastoral Care of the Sick: Rites of Anointing and Viaticum* (Ottawa: Canadian Conference of Catholic Bishops, 1983). See also the reference in Gusmer, *And You Visited Me*, 191.

[20] See n. 5 above.

[21] John M. Huels, "Ministers and Rites for the Sick and Dying: Canon Law and Pastoral Options," *Recovering the Riches of Anointing: A Study of the Sacrament of the Sick*, 89–90.

[22] "The spiritual effects of sacramentals, unlike those of sacraments, are realized not through the action itself *(ex opere operato)* but by way of intercession (Can. 1166). Prayer should always accompany the use of blessed objects, lest they be reduced to magical talismans" (ibid., 93).

[23] Specifically the "Order of Blessing of the Sick" in the *Book of Blessings*. He cites the 1987 translation and adaptation by ICEL of *De benedictionibus* (*editio typica* of 1984).

[24] Huels, "Ministers and Rites for the Sick and Dying," 95. His footnote no. 30 on the same page presents the text of the blessing from *The Roman Ritual: Complete Edition*, ed. Philip T. Weller (Milwaukee: Bruce, 1964) 573.

[25] See Robert Murray, *Symbols of Church and Kingdom* (London: Cambridge University Press, 1975).

[26] See the similar discussion in Michael Drumm, "The Practice of Anointing and the Development of Doctrine," in *Recovering the Riches of Anointing*, especially pp. 37–38.

[27] Thomas Talley's wonderful essay on anointing of the sick, "Healing: Sacrament or Charism" (*Worship* 46 [1972] 518–27), reprinted in *Reforming Tradition* (Washington, D.C.: The Pastoral Press, 1990) 47–58, describes it best by noting that the ministers (presbyters) are called primarily as representatives of the community, "summoned as the constitutive representatives of the community, not as *thaumatourgoi*, nor even as *sacerdotes*. Their function is not to heal nor is it yet to administer last rites, but to protect the sick member from dereliction and separation from the ecclesial body" (p. 52).

[28] The whole body of Christ gathered together, outwardly symbolized by the various orders in the Church (beginning with the rank of laity), is a hallmark of Eastern Christian thought. One of its finest articulations is by John Zizioulas, *Being as Communion: Studies in Personhood and the Church* (Crestwood, NY: St. Vladimir's Seminary Press, 1997), in which he states: "there is no such thing as non-ordained persons in the church," pp. 215–16. See also the discussion in Susan K. Wood, "The Paschal Mystery: The Intersection of Ecclesiology and Sacramental Theology in the Care of the Sick" in *Recovering the Riches of Anointing: A Study of the Sacrament of the Sick*, especially pp. 11–19, and Richard R. Gaillardetz, "The Ecclesiological Foundations of Ministry within an Ordered Communion," *Ordering the Baptismal Priesthood: Theologies of Lay and Ordained Ministry*, ed. Susan K. Wood (Collegeville: Liturgical Press, 2003) 26–51.

[29] "Dogmatic Constitution on the Church," Vatican II, *Lumen Gentium*, 21 November 1964.

[30] See Susan K. Wood, *Sacramental Orders* (Collegeville: Liturgical Press, 2000) especially ch. 1.

[31] See the discussion in Wood, "The Paschal Mystery: The Intersection of Ecclesiology and Sacramental Theology in the Care of the Sick," p. 12, with reference to Thomas Talley's article, "Healing: Sacrament or Charism?"

[32] Council of Trent, 14th Session, Canon 4. *Decrees of the Ecumenical Councils*, vol. 2, ed. Norman P. Tanner (Washington D.C.: Georgetown University Press, 1995).

[33] John J. Ziegler, *Let Them Anoint the Sick* (Collegeville: Liturgical Press, 1987) especially ch. 8.

[34] Rather than only issues of heretical content, much of the writings of the Council of Trent surrounding the presented articles and the theological responses were concerned with the challenges contrary to the practices of the Church. Regarding the specific debate over extreme unction, Ziegler writes " . . . the theologians claimed that the Protestant articles were heretical, not because their content opposed divine revelation, but because the teaching was contrary to the understanding and practice of the Church. Therefore, even though some of them assigned to one or the other article the theological note "false," they were unanimous in their decision that both articles should be condemned as heretical because they were against the understanding of the Church" (*Let Them Anoint the Sick*, 123).

[35] This would seem to be the approach taken in *Dominicae Cenae*, particularly in Section I: "The Eucharist is the principal and central *raison d'etre* of the sacrament of the priesthood . . . in a certain way we derive from it and exist for it" (Letter of John Paul II to Priests on Holy Thursday).

[36] Thomas O'Meara summarizes the "five basic theological (liturgical and ecclesial) changes" that Henri Denis described as crucial to understanding the movement from Trent to Vatican I: "First, the point of departure for subsequent changes was expanding the understanding of the mission of the Church from the priest's celebration of the Eucharist (joined to the congregation at the time of Communion) to a fuller mission of the Church. Second, Denis thinks that the recent council sees the institution of the priesthood not to be found solely at the Last Supper but in Jesus' institution of apostles and disciples, apostolate and ministry. Third, the specificity of the presbyter is not solely in the power to consecrate bread and wine but to act in various ways in the power of the risen Christ, precisely for and in Christ as the head of his body. Fourth, the priesthood is essentially ministerial: it is not solely cultic but flows from the ministry of the apostles and active ministers announcing the Gospel and founding churches. Finally, the relationship of the presbyter to God does not occur in celebratory isolation during the words of consecration, but that action and all that he does is bound to God's grace in the life and context of a fuller ministry of the pastor" (Thomas O'Meara, "The Ministry of Presbyters and the Many Ministries in the Church," *The Theology of Priesthood*, ed. Donald J. Goergen and Ann Garrido [Collegeville: Liturgical Press, 2000] 71–72).

[37] " . . . catechesis should emphasize that regardless of who administers the anointing, it is a liturgical celebration of faith of the entire Christian community. The medievalists were correct in observing that the prayer of the sacraments is a public prayer and should be led by a public person. Today the ontological change that results from ordination to hierarchical orders tends to be understood relationally. Whether

ordination is to the presbyteral or diaconal office, the ordained person, by virtue of his permanent commitment and the public call and acceptance of the Church, not only assumes the identity of being a public person in the Christian community but is also recognized as being charged with the responsibility of exercising in the Church's name its official ministry" (Ziegler, *Let Them Anoint the Sick*, 152).

[38] See Wood, *Sacramental Orders*, especially chs. 4 and 5.

[39] See particularly *The Catechism of the Catholic Church and Christifideles Laici: Post-Synodal Exhortation of His Holiness John Paul II* (1988).

[40] Paul Philibert, "Issues for a Theology of Priesthood: A Status Report," *The Theology of Priesthood*, 36.

[41] See the volume on the sacrament of reconciliation in this series, David M. Coffey, *The Sacrament of Reconciliation* (Collegeville: Liturgical Press, 2001).

[42] Again, for the details on the scholastic differentiation, particularly between Franciscan and Dominican theologians, see the Coffey volume on reconciliation.

[43] "The association of anointing with the forgiveness of sin, despite its long history with the sacrament of reconciliation, belongs more to the metaphor system surrounding the word 'salvation' than to the forensic metaphor of 'justification,' although both are juxtaposed in Jesus' ministry" (Wood, "The Paschal Mystery," 5–6).

[44] See Paragraph 6 of the General Introduction.

[45] Peter Fink, "Anointing of the Sick and the Forgiveness of Sins," *Recovering the Riches of Anointing*, 33.

[46] Although some theologians have complained that the current formula is still too vague, when compared to the previous formula of the Roman Ritual, "May the Lord forgive you by this holy anointing and his most loving mercy whatever sins you committed by the use of your sight . . . ," it is clearly a move towards seeing the effects of anointing as more than simply the forgiveness of sins. *A New Commentary on the Code of Canon Law*, ed. John P. Beal, James A. Coriden, and Thomas J. Green (New York: Paulist Press, 2000) 998–99.

[47] Pope Paul VI: "Here as in the other sacraments the Church's main concern is, of course, the increase of God's grace. But also, to the extent that it is up to the Church, its desire and intent is to obtain relief and, if possible, even healing for the sick . . . " (Homily, October 5, 1975, Documents on the Liturgy [1975] 412, p. 1062).

[48] Although, see Thomas Talley's article on this distinction between sacramental and charismatic healing, between ecclesial action and extraordinary miracle, in which he cautions against too broad a division (particularly 47–50).

[49] See, for example, the general histories of sacraments such as those found in Joseph Martos, *Doors to the Sacred: A Historical Introduction to Sacraments in the Catholic Church* (Tarrytown, NY: Triumph Books, 1991) 321–25; Herbert Vorgrimler, *Sacramental Theology* (Collegeville: Liturgical Press, 1992) 228–29; William J. Bausch, *A New Look at the Sacraments* (Mystic, CT: Twenty-Third Publications, 1983) 202–06; and Michael G. Lawler, *Symbol and Sacrament: A Contemporary Sacramental Theology* (Omaha, NE: Creighton University Press, 1995) 162–63.

[50] " . . . Rome is cautious about referring to the priest's status *in persona Ecclesiae*, since "it would make the priest simply a delegate of the community." As Coffey says, it is "desirable for the priest to be a delegate of the community in some

sense, but it is more important that he be called by God and appointed by legitimate authority" (David Coffey, "Priestly Representation and Women's Ordination," *Priesthood: The Hard Questions,* ed. Gerald Gleeson, 80; cited in Paul Philibert's article, "Issues for a Theology of Priesthood: A Status Report," 30). The issue of the priest acting *in persona ecclesiae* and *in persona Christi* continues to be foundational to restrictions on the minister of the anointing of the sick. See the 11 February 2005 Doctrinal Congregation Note, "Only Priests May Administer the Anointing of the Sick," which reiterates this restriction and declares that it is a doctrine definitively held *(definitive tenenda)* for several reasons, including "in the administration of the Sacraments, the priest acts *in persona Christi capitis* and *in persona ecclesiae . . . ." Origins* 34:42 (April 7, 2005) 673.

[51] See Philibert, "Issues for a Theology of Priesthood."

[52] Philibert, "Issues for a Theology of Priesthood," 31.

[53] Coffey and others will argue for the preeminence of ascending theology in sacramental theology in a similar vein as in biblical (New Testament) theology with regard to *in persona Ecclesiae*: "Yet taking the perspective of an ascending theology, *in persona Ecclesiae* is seen as an indispensable prerequisite, a foundation of the condition of action *in persona Christi. In persona Ecclesiae* is a necessary stage toward of the acquisition of the status of one acting *in persona Christi"* (Philibert, "Issues for a Theology of Priesthood," 31). This, of course, puts the discussion into a different realm than the baptized Christian who stands as the person of Christ in the world and within the body of Christ as participant.

[54] What is not present in this argument is the essential nature of baptism versus anointing of the sick. That argument is somewhat nuanced in recent liturgical reforms (particularly the "Order of Christian Funerals," which makes no judgment on the death of an unbaptized infant).

[55] In 2003, the report listed 44,487 priests (including semi-retired) and 66,407,105 Roman Catholics in the United States. In some of the western states the statistical imbalance is more obvious. For example, the Archdiocese of Los Angeles reports only 1,141 active priests and 4,206,875 active Roman Catholics. See *The Official Catholic Directory* (New York: Kennedy and Sons, 2003) 2144.

[56] NACC (National Association of Catholic Chaplains). Their mission statements reads: "The National Association of Catholic Chaplains is a professional association for certified chaplains and clinical pastoral educators who participate in the healing mission of Jesus Christ. We provide standards, certification, education, advocacy and professional development for our members in service to the Church and society" (from the website at www.nacc.org).

[57] Joseph J. Driscoll, "Foreword," *Recovering the Richs of Anointing,* viii.

[58] This is particularly apparent in "Survey Results: Analysis of Written Comments," NACC *Survey on the Sacrament of the Anointing of the Sick* (Edwin Fonner, Jr., Dr Ph, 1995) especially pp. 7–11.

[59] Kevin Tripp and Genevieve Glen, "Introduction," *Recovering the Riches of Anointing,* xiii.

[60] Cited in the Introduction of John J. Ziegler's *Let Them Anoint the Sick,* 1.

[61] Ibid., 2.

[62] See n. 57 above.

[63] Driscoll, "Foreword," viii.

[64] NACC Survey, "Problems Experienced by Respondents," particularly notes problems in rural areas, such as too few priests, too great a distance between parish and hospital, too much time between call to priest and his arrival, etc. See pp. 7–10.

[65] See paragraph 99 of the *praenotanda* of the Anointing of the Sick (Chapter IV): "The priest should ensure that the abuse of delaying the reception of the sacrament does not occur, and that the celebration takes place while the sick person is capable of active participation. However, the intent of the Conciliar reform (Constitution on the Sacred Liturgy, 73) that those needing the sacrament should seek it at the beginning of a serious illness should not be used to anoint those who are not proper subjects for the sacrament. The sacrament of the anointing of the sick *should be celebrated only when a Christian's health is seriously impaired by sickness or old age*" (italics mine).

[66] This issue was discussed briefly in ch. 1 above, but follows on the footnotes of paragraph 8 in the General Introduction: "The word *periculose* has been carefully studied and rendered as 'seriously,' rather than as 'gravely,' 'dangerously,' or 'perilously.' Such a rendering will serve to avoid restrictions upon the celebration of the sacrament. On the one hand, the sacrament may and should be given to anyone whose health is seriously impaired; on the other hand, it may not be given indiscriminately or to any person whose health is not seriously impaired."

[67] See paragraph 108 which responds to perceived abuses in communal anointing circumstances: "In particular, the practice of indiscriminately anointing numbers of people on these occasions simply because they are ill or have reached an advanced age is to be avoided. Only those whose health is seriously impaired by sickness or old age are proper subjects for the sacraments." See also John M. Huels, "Who May Be Anointed," *Disputed Questions*, 91–99.

[68] David Power, "The Sacrament of Anointing: Open Questions," 101. Power is drawing on the interpretive work of Giorgio Gozzelino, *L'Unzione degli Infermi, Sacramento della Vittoria sulla Malattia* (Turin, 1970) 157–61.

[69] See Charles Gusmer, *And You Visited Me: Sacramental Ministry to the Sick and the Dying*, rev. ed. (New York: Pueblo Publishing Co., 1989) especially ch. 4; Talley, "Healing: Sacrament or Charism?"

[70] Michael Drumm, "The Practice of Anointing and the Development of Doctrine," 49.

[71] Huel, "Who May Be Anointed," 91–99.

[72] See James L. Empereur, *Prophetic Anointing: God's Call to the Sick, the Elderly, and the Dying* (Wilmington, DE: Michael Glazier, 1986) especially ch. 5.

[73] Probably the best example of the seriousness of lasting obligations is the charge found in many Roman Pontificals of the twelfth century: "The priest says to the sick man: 'Why have you summoned me, brother?' 'That you may anoint me.' The priest says: 'May our Lord Jesus Christ bestow on you a genuine and easy anointing; but if the Lord looks upon you and heals you, will you preserve the anointing?' 'I will preserve it'" (cited in A. G. Martimort, "Prayer for the Sick and Sacramental Anointing," *The Church at Prayer:* Vol. III: *The Sacraments* [Collegeville: Liturgical Press, 1988] 131).

[74] Paragraph 14, italics mine.

[75] Paragraph 7, italics mine.

[76] "Mother Church earnestly desires that all the faithful should be led to that full, conscious, and active participation in liturgical celebrations which is demanded by the very nature of the liturgy, and to which the Christian people, 'a chosen race, a royal priesthood, a holy nation, a redeemed people' (1 Pet. 2:9, 4-5) have a right and obligation by reason of their baptism" (CSL, 14).

[77] See above, n. 8.

[78] Talley, "Healing: Sacrament or Charism?", 55.

[79] Susan Wood, "The Paschal Mystery," 7.

[80] Mary Collins, "The Roman Ritual: Pastoral Care and Anointing of the Sick," 13.

[81] Ibid.

[82] Ibid., 12.

[83] See Kenan Osborne, *Christian Sacraments in a Postmodern World: A Theology for the Third Millennium* (New York: Paulist Press, 1999) 70.

[84] Ibid., 149.

[85] Edward Cothenet, "Healing as a Sign of the Kingdom and the Anointing of the Sick," *Temple of the Holy Spirit: Sickness and Death of the Christian in the Liturgy:* 21st Liturgical Conference, Saint-Serge (New York: Pueblo Publishing Co., 1983) 48.

[86] Ibid., 38–39.

[87] M. Jennifer Glen, "Sickness and Symbol: The Promise of the Future," *Worship* 54 (1981) 410.

[88] Ibid.

[89] Ibid., 410–11.

[90] "Open Questions," 101ff.

[91] Gusmer, *And You Visited Me*, 148.

[92] Talley, "Healing: Sacrament or Charism?", 49.

[93] Gusmer, *And You Visited Me*, 139–45.

[94] Jennifer Glen describes these same 'categories' of alienation as "intrapersonal," "interpersonal," and "transpersonal," arriving at similar conclusions to Charles Gusmer. See "Rites of Healing: A Reflection in Pastoral Theology," *Alternative Futures for Worship*, vol. 7: *Anointing of the Sick*, ed. Peter. E. Fink (Collegeville: Liturgical Press, 1987) 40–43.

[95] Mary Collins "The Roman Ritual: Pastoral Care and Anointing of the Sick," 10, 16–17.

[96] "Co-suffering" is an apt description by Jennifer Glen, in her article "Rites of Healing: A Reflection in Pastoral Theology," 47.

[97] Here the author relies on personal experience as a hospital chaplain at UCSF medical center and on the anecdotal responses associated with the 1994 survey from the USCC white paper to the American bishops.

[98] There have been many interesting studies of inculturated healing rites in Africa because of the recognition of a more holistic view of the human person at the root of the often-syncretistic rites, as well as the communal understanding of the implications of health and sickness. See Meinrad Hebga, "Healing in Africa," *The Pastoral Care of the Sick,* 60–71, for a brief overview.

[99] See Frederick S. Paxton, *Christianizing Death: The Creation of a Ritual Process in Early Medieval Europe* (Ithaca: Cornell University Press, 1990) especially ch. 1;

and *The Oil of Gladness: Anointing in the Christian Tradition*, ed. Martin Dudley and Geoffrey Rowell (London: SPCK, 1993) especially chs. 4 and 6.

[100] See Basilius Groen, "The Anointing of the Sick in the Greek Orthodox Church," *The Pastoral Care of the Sick*, 50–59.

[101] Cor Traets, "The Sick and Suffering Person: A Liturgical/Sacramental Approach," *God and Human Suffering*, ed. Jan Lambrecht and Raymond F. Collins (Louvain: Peeters Press, 1989) 184.

[102] Talley, "Healing: Sacrament or Charism?", 53.

[103] Gusmer, *And You Visited Me*, 147.

[104] Talley, "Healing: Sacrament or Charism?", 50.

[105] See Glen, "Sickness and Symbol," 397–411.

[106] Nathan Mitchell, *Real Presence: The Work of Eucharist* (Chicago: LTP, 1998) 98–100.

[107] The famous phrase of Pope Leo the Great still remains the best summation: "What was visible of the Lord has passed over into the sacraments."

[108] Osborne, *Christian Sacraments in a Postmodern World*, 142–45.

[109] Ibid., 82.

[110] Gusmer, *And You Visited Me*, 149.

[111] David N. Power, "Let the Sick Call," *Culture and Theology* (Washington, D.C.: The Pastoral Press, 1990) 249.

[112] The essential trinitarian nature of all sacramental action (and all theology) and in particular, the restoration of the centrality of the role of the Holy Spirit, has been an important part of the liturgical movement from Congar to the new Catechism. A summary of Congar's theology states that he "maintains that the constitutive act of invoking the Holy Spirit in the sacraments is not confined to formal epicletic phrases but permeates the entire liturgical event . . . . In the sacraments, the Spirit neither reveals nor asserts himself, but points 'back' to the Father who has been revealed through the Son, and 'ahead' to the Son who will hand over all things to the Father. . . . In the context of this trinitarian perspective, the liturgical epiclesis reveals two fundamental movements. On the one hand, the Spirit creates a centripetal movement by drawing the recipients of the sacraments towards internal unity. On the other hand, the same Spirit makes the unity of the community that is formed in and through sacramental reception a relational one oriented towards the whole of creation" (Isaac Kizhakkeparampil, *The Invocation of the Holy Spirit as Constitutive of the Sacraments According to Cardinal Yves Congar* [Roma: Editrice Pontificia Universita Gregoriana, 1995] 167–68). Congar's work, while often focused on eucharistic liturgy, exemplifies the sacramental effect of overcoming alienation in the anointing of the sick through his exposition of trinitarian cooperation. See Isaac Kizhakkeparampil, *The Invocation of the Holy Spirit as Constitutive of the Sacraments According to Cardinal Yves Congar* (Roma: Editrice Pontificia Universita Gregoriana, 1995) 167–68.

[113] Traets, "The Sick and Suffering Person," *God and Human Suffering*, 185.

[114] Glen, "Rites of Healing: A Reflection in Pastoral Theology," 38.

[115] Ibid., 39.

[116] Power, "Open Questions," 104.

Chapter Four

The Contexts of Church and Culture for Pastoral Care of the Sick

In the previous chapter, the classic issues of matter and form, minister, subject, and sacramental efficacy with regard to anointing of the sick were re-examined and found fruitful in raising new and continuing questions. In this chapter, we will look at other questions raised by the rite and its interaction with the larger Church and world. As the rite has been used, prayed, and relied on in the past twenty years, patients, families, chaplains, priests, and students have interacted with the written word and rubrical instructions of the rite in health care, Church, cultural, and theological settings, all of which have undergone extensive and rapid changes in the same time period. Each experience of the sacrament of the anointing is both unique and in communion with all other sacramental encounters, so the contexts in which the rite in its fullest possibilities (the entire *Pastoral Care of the Sick*) and in the specificity of the sacrament of *The Anointing of the Sick* actually happen increasingly challenge assumptions about how the language is heard or the rite is perceived and received by those engaging in it.

In this chapter we will look at four related and organic issues that are influencing the Church's ministry to the sick. The first issue is the relationship between professional health care and pastoral ministry to the sick. In the last two decades there have been tremendous advances in the technical abilities of the medical world to prolong and save lives at the same time as discernable changes have appeared in the relationship between medicine and spirituality. Both of these impact the way pastoral care is approached and will form the basis for two different discussions in this chapter.

A contributing factor to the change in the relationship between medicine and spirituality is culture, specifically a trans-ethnic inculturation of healing in many parts of the United States. This second context of culture has also had an impact on the reception of the anointing the sick in ways not addressed or predicted by the rite. The continued health of the rite of anointing of the sick as it is practiced and handed down to another generation cannot help but be affected by an increasingly pluralistic world and its views on ritual, Christian spirituality, and the relationship of people and practices of other faiths.

The third issue impacting pastoral care of the sick is not new, but is rather an ongoing context into which culture and health care are bringing new questions. This is the theological understanding of human suffering and how shifts in treatment and cultural assumptions have overtly and subtly influenced the perception of the language of the rite at the same time that the rite itself has influenced theological understandings of suffering.

Finally, the fourth issue, intimately related to health care, culture, and the theology of suffering is the pastoral care of the dying. Earlier chapters of this work have advocated for the contemporary rite and its primacy as the sacrament of the sick, not of the dying, but the contextual changes listed immediately above beg that the question of pastoral care of the dying be raised again, not so much as a rebuttal, but as a question to be studied in light of the *Anointing of the Sick* as an example of the Church in the modern world. Each section will begin with citations from appropriate paragraphs of the General Introduction to *Pastoral Care of the Sick*.

Spirituality, Faith, and Medicine

Part of the plan laid out by God's providence is that we should fight strenuously against all sickness and carefully seek the blessings of good health, so that we may fulfill our role in human society and in the Church (PCS 3).

The sick person is not the only one who should fight against illness. Doctors and all who are devoted in any way to caring for the sick

should consider it their duty to use all the means which in their judgment may help the sick, both physically and spiritually. In so doing,
they are fulfilling the command of Christ to visit the sick, for Christ
implied that those who visit the sick should be concerned for the
whole person and offer both physical relief and spiritual comfort
(PCS 4).

Every scientific effort to prolong life and every act of care for the
sick, on the part of any person, may be considered a preparation for
the Gospel and a sharing in Christ's healing ministry (PCS 32).

The family and friends of the sick, doctors and others who care for
them, and priests with pastoral responsibilities have a particular share
in this ministry of comfort (PCS 43).

Hospital personnel (doctors, nurses, aides) should also be prepared to
exercise a special role with the [dying] child as caring adults. Priests
and deacons bear particular responsibility for overseeing all these elements of the Church's pastoral ministry (PCS 170).

The paragraphs cited above reveal not only a charge to the patient to
do all in his or her power to maintain health, but also state a presumption that the professional health specialists will do all in their power to
help the sick physically and spiritually, caring for the whole person.
This unity of purpose among different constituencies has not always
been this clear. The particular history of the relationship between medicine and spirituality has been inconsistent and varied, with a pattern of
cooperation and competition seemingly alternating as the views of the
human person and the relationship between sin and sickness evolved or
devolved.

The cultural/religious world into which Christianity was born had
multiple sources for understanding medicine as more an aspect of religion than not. From Judaism came stories of healing, signs, and wonders, with the God of creation often presented as healer,[1] but few
positive references to physicians (Gen 50:1-3 stands alone in the core
of Hebrew scripture). Not until the writing of Sirach is the physician
seen as a valuable co-worker with God. "Instead of being portrayed as
an opponent of God, the physician is said to have been created by God
and to have provided the medicines 'out of the earth' which sensible
people will welcome and utilize."[2] Besides this praise for the skills of
the physician, however, there is still an understanding that "prayer and
sacrifice are essential for the efficacy of healing," and that "the link be-

tween sickness and sin is explicit."[3] This shift in understanding the physician and the medical arts in a positive light has been attributed to the "influence of the Greek tradition of medicine" at a time of intense Hellenistic influence on Judaism,[4] and it is from that Greek tradition of medicine that the greatest positive (and lasting) influences emerged.

Ancient Greek medicine is understood as possessing "no cleft between medicine and the ministrations of the gods"; medicine and religion were intertwined.[5] The Hippocratic tradition (whether from Hippocrates or not) made use of evidence discerned and reviewed about the whole person, including what we would today call a combination of physical, psychological, social, and spiritual analyses.[6]

While the New Testament does not say a great deal about human physicians, the centrality of Jesus as healer imbued the imagery of physician with positive associations. The early Church, however, did not generally present the medical arts as strongly negative or positive. In most references, they were simply there, and as long as their historical association with the gods was set aside or at least not overt, there was limited animosity toward the healing arts in the first few centuries of Christianity. In some cases prominent Christian leaders saw the work of pastors and physicians as one of mutual ministry.

> Humanity is the regular business of all you who practice as physicians. And, in my opinion, to put your science at the head and front of life's pursuits is to decide reasonably and rightly. This at all events seems to be the case if man's most precious possession, life, is painful and not worth living, unless it be lived in health, and if for health we are dependent upon your skill. In your own case medicine is seen, as it were, with two right hands; you enlarge the accepted limits of philanthropy by not confining the application of your skills to men's bodies, but by attending also to the cure of the diseases of their souls. It is not only in accordance with popular report that I thus write. I am moved by the personal experience which I have had on many occasions.[7]

St. Basil's letter to a physician friend in the 380s represented the most positive of Christian views on medicine and those who made their living by practicing it. Far from his urban Christian world of Asia Minor, however, a different view was emerging in the Western Church. There, the world of medical experts was increasingly seen as competition, and faith best expressed by shunning all but the Church's healing. In the sixth century, Caesarius of Arles, concerned with the magical undertones of herbal medicine, amulets, and folk medicine, urged his parishioners, especially the women who cared for the sick at home, to put their trust in the Eucharist and blessed oil:

> How much more correct and salutary it would be to hurry to the church, to receive the body and blood of Christ, and with oil that is blessed to anoint in all faith themselves and their dear ones; for according to what James the Apostle says, not only would they receive health of body, but also remission of sins.[8]

Caesarius' distrust of indigenous medical practices is benign compared to his contemporary Gregory of Tours. For Gregory, the relics of saints and martyrs, especially newly discovered local heroes, were the real medicine, and one sees with his approach an animosity toward any other methods of healing that might challenge or compete with these manifestations of the will of God. His championing of the local healing cults under his episcopal control was joined to a widespread fatalism in an era of frequent wars and illness. In this setting, a person would recover only if God willed it and only by miraculous means. There was little room in Gregory's world for a naturalism that allowed another way of explaining sickness and health.

> Gregory's choice of enemies throws into high relief the content of his belief that life made sense in terms of a Catholic *reverentia*. For these enemies are the bearers of alternative systems of explanation—the soothsayer, the folk-doctor and (quite as important for Gregory, because also the bearer of a rival system of cure and explanation) the Christian popular prophet.[9]

A variety of opinions and degrees of animosity towards medicine characterized the first millennium of Christianity, which coincided with an overall decline (in the West) in the knowledge of medical arts. The skills of surgery and classical medical knowledge were unknown in many medieval circles and this contributed to the virtual disappearance of the normative lay physician. At the same time, however, the retention of some of that classical knowledge in monastic libraries and the continuing necessity of practicing pastoral medicine promoted the shift of medicine to the monastic world and changed the emphasis and medicinal approach. It was in the monasteries that much of the indigenous herbal medical knowledge was preserved, as well as the continuation of the hospice tradition. This resulted in an interesting relationship between theology and medicine where the normative physician was also a priest, the medieval *medicina clericalis*.[10]

It would not be until the renaissance of theological thinking in the twelfth and thirteenth centuries that a more systematic approach to medicine would appear in the realm of ethics or moral theology, an approach that opened up greater levels of cooperation between the fields. That this renaissance was not limited to theology alone was exemplified by the birth of medical schools such as that at Salerno, where "large numbers of secular physicians" were trained for the first time in a number of centuries.[11]

> Whereas often in previous centuries there had been a battle between medical practice and religious remedies, and medical techniques had been opposed as usurpations of God's power, now the scholastic notions of nature, secondary causality, and "necessitas ex suppositione" enabled Christians to view such interventions as part of God's providence for humankind rather than as attacks against it.[12]

These lay physicians, still very much part of the Christian theocentric world of their time, could now use their "God-given and God-approved skills . . . in service of [their] patients."[13]

The first extant theological treatise that took advantage of the twelfth century renaissance of medical knowledge was focused on reproductive medicine and ethics. In Paulo Zacchia's *Quaestiones medio-legales* from the mid-seventeenth century, the central discussion (and the one for which he is remembered as a primary contributor) was "his opinion that the ensoulment of a fetus takes place at fertilization."[14] Zacchia's three volume work summarized the state of medical ethics at the time and paved the way for what would later be called "Pastoral Medicine" (an eighteenth-century term). His treatment of the topic from both the medical and theological perspectives would stand as somewhat unique, however, and the shape of the field to come was perhaps better represented by Michael Boudewyns, whose 1666 work is "restricted to the presentation of moral theological opinion concerning the practice of medicine."[15] In other words, it was first and foremost a manual for theologians and confessors to understand the world of physicians and medicine in order to advise the latter. The relationship between theology and the Church on one side, and the world of physicians and medical advances on the other, were both the concerns of the emerging field of pastoral medicine, but usually one professional area was dominant at any given time and in any particular work. Either the emphasis was on medicine in order to aid theologians in their understanding, or the emphasis was on ethics and canon law, in order to aid Catholic physicians in their decision-making.

In spite of this, the cooperative approach (at least within the world of Roman Catholicism) remained until the Enlightenment, at which time a number of fundamental philosophical changes, including a shift from the dominant theocentric worldview to one that was more anthropocentric, influenced the field of medicine. In spite of that substantial cultural and philosophical shift, the relationship between the Church and medicine continued to flourish, with writings falling roughly into three categories. First there were medical primers for rural priests and missionaries enabling them to perform rudimentary procedures in lieu of any available physicians, not so much theology as functional substitution (the priest as doctor, *medicina ruralis*).[16] Second, there were the writings that tried to clericalize (and romanticize) the role of doctor, until their moral, life-making decisions sounded very much like the work of a confessor (the doctor as priest).[17] Third, there were the scholarly volumes that addressed the intersection of the fields of medicine and theology in a more evenhanded way. The early nineteenth-century work by Angelo Scotti can stand as exemplar of this category. In his three sections "he speaks first of the benefits which medicine has received from religion, second of the service medicine can offer to religion, and third of the obligations which religion prescribes for medicine."[18] It is this latter which will mark the primary thrust of the field in the nineteenth and twentieth centuries with the emphasis on "the authority of religion to determine the moral obligations of physicians" and the physician's "obligation never to advise a patient contrary to moral law."[19]

In addition to the authoritative directives from moral theologians, one is struck by the consistency of the scope of concerns in the nineteenth and early twentieth century works. The Church's directives were increasingly limited to reproductive medicine, with the areas of euthanasia and mutilation a distant second and third. As the speed of medical advances snowballed in the latter half of the nineteenth and into the early decades of the twentieth century, the Church's approach to medicine became less open, perhaps as part of a delayed reaction to the medical world's rejection of theocentrism as a working model of the world.

The perception of the twin dangers of materialism and modernism became influential at the same time as the rapid growth of Catholic hospitals in the United States and the emergence of a network of cooperation between those hospitals and the training of medical professionals to staff them.[20] These realities resulted in an unfortunate oversimplification that pitted faith (Catholic) against reason (the medical profession),[21] which in turn, led to a hardening of positions. The dominant voices in medical ethics/moral theology in these first decades of the twentieth century often did not help the situation of animosity either. Alexander Sanford, in his *Pastoral Medicine*, addressing the quandary of having to choose between saving a mother or an unborn child, states that the "blame" is with the mother, not the innocent child.

> Even if the child cannot be born without imperiling the life of its mother, it is more than doubtful whether the child can be regarded as committing the assault. In by far the largest number of cases the impediment is caused by the mother; for instance, by a too narrow pelvis, etc. Besides, the act of giving birth has not its origin with the child, but with the mother. The danger for mother and child comes from the action of the womb, which, while not controlled by the mother's will-power emanates from her, pertains to her. Hence, if by a voluntary act on the part of the mother, by procreation, the child without any of its own doing has been placed within the mother's womb . . . and if all these circumstances, all due to the mother, tend to jeopardize the lives of mother and child, can anyone possessed of a particle of justice maintain that the child has committed an unjust assault, or even an assault? . . . Therefore artificial abortion is to be looked upon as an unjustifiable homicide; it is tantamount to murder.[22]

Charles J. McFadden, in his *Medical Ethics for Nurses,* advocates against euthanasia for reasons that sound inappropriate to modern readers:

> The advocates of euthanasia moreover disregard the supernatural destiny of man and the role which suffering can play in the achievement of sanctity. They do not realize the ability of man, aided by God's grace, to bear sufferings patiently. They do not know how resignation to pain can serve as penance and temporal punishment for personal moral failing. Lacking a true belief in the supernatural, they have no respect for the power of faith and prayer to produce miracles in even the most hopeless cases.[23]

The spiritual profitability of pain leads McFadden to forbid "the giving of pain-relieving drugs which cause unconsciousness to those 'dying in great pain without being spiritually prepared for death.'"[24] In spite of these historically unpalatable opinions, however, some of these early authors have been seriously ill-used by contemporary writers to set up a further polemic between religion and medical practice.[25]

Moralists with a narrow spectrum of interests were not, however, the only voices in the early decades of the twentieth century. There was another school of pastoral medicine or dialogue between theology and medicine emerging which took the best of an historical approach from both schools and began to emphasize wellness and wholeness as a notable contribution of theology to the medical field. These theologians and physicians emphasized care for the whole person as integral to both health on the one hand, and salvation on the other, and led the way for some fundamental shifts in the training and work of medical professionals.

Emerging from this cooperative work of the mid-twentieth century, there has been an explosion of writing on the topic of medicine and spirituality in the past ten to fifteen years especially, and the growing consensus is that spirituality is good for your health.[26] Behind this facile statement are radical shifts in the way that medicine views the world of spirituality, at least in the United States and in a number of other countries as well. In 1992 only five medical schools in this country had a course on the relationship between traditional religious beliefs and health, as compared with over sixty schools by 2000.[27] That alone represents a "mainstreaming" of the fundamental concept of approaching the whole person in order to facilitate healing. Physician Dana King traces the evolution of how the sick are approached, presenting three historical "models" that exemplify the growing dialogue between medicine and spirituality. He calls the first model the "biomedical model," "based on a seventeenth century scientific worldview characterized by reductionism, mechanistic thinking, and mind-body dualism."[28] In many ways this is the classic paradigm of medical evaluation, and practitioners of this approach are still in evidence in many places. Paul Philibert assumes the dominance of this approach when he writes, "contemporary medicine is inclined to establish a relational distance between the caregiver and the patient, on the one hand, and to create a typology of disease from similar cases despite the uniqueness of the persons afflicted."[29] The characteristic difference between "curing" and "healing" comes into play here, with curing being the isolation of the sickness and a focus on isolated symptoms or injuries, as opposed to healing which addresses the whole person in the work of becoming whole.[30]

This biomedical model has been challenged over the past twenty-five years with the development and refinement of the "biopsychosocial model," which has emerged "in response to much research on the influence of psychosocial factors, family, support, and stress on the biology of health . . . what was once a provocative idea has evolved into a widely accepted concept that [these] factors can affect health and illness."[31] While this model for patient care has much to commend it because of advantages over the biomedical model, Dana King and others are convinced that a further model has not only been helpful in use with patients but needs to be advocated much more strongly because the biopsychosocial model "does not recognize explicitly the influence of religious commitment and spirituality on health."[32] Their proposal is a "biopsychospiritual model," which would "add the spiritual dimension to the current biopsychosocial model and would include spirituality with God, nature, the inner self, or other beliefs that provide meaning to patients' lives."[33] Contrary to some opinions from the medical world, they felt that "taking into account patients' spirituality is not 'alternative' medicine. It demonstrates sensitivity to an integral part of the whole person, a part that exists independently from considerations of health and illness."[34]

The remainder of King's study cites the many tests that have been run on different groups of patients to support the theory that weekly attendance at religious services, prayer, intrinsic beliefs, and religious practices do make a difference in overall health and particularly in recovery rates. Enough of these studies have been carried out that the book market of physicians advocating for an "epidemiology of religion"[35] is widespread and ongoing. Many of these studies offer concrete suggestions for "taking a spiritual history" which would give physicians insight into patients' beliefs and help physicians develop sensitivity to religious and cultural issues.[36] Most of the texts available, however, are cautious about overstating the achievements of collaboration between medical experts, sensitive and willing to engage in religious discussions, and the "experts," here usually presented as hospital chaplains. While praising the professionalism of chaplains (one chapter read like an *apologia* for the training and graduate education of clergy chaplains in particular[37]), the physician authors admitted there was still a low percentage of statistical proof that this type of cooperation was widespread. This "integration gap" of collaboration between chaplains and physicians was noted in several books. "Only 22% [of physicians] reported using referrals to chaplains or other spiritual leaders in more than 10% of encounters."[38] Statistics like these were transparently frustrating to many of the authors concerned with expanding the cooperation for the good of the patient and remained as a primary impetus for the continuing statistical work of how spirituality (through the concrete means of these very types of cooperation) benefited the patient.

While these and other statistics confirm the missionary status of much of the work from within the field of health care, the advocacy for collaboration from the side of the churches has not been as strong as one would think. Too often discussions on the teamwork necessary to enable the overall health of the patient have taken a back seat to internal Church squabbles or fears of nurses as spiritual leaders taking away from the "experts." And too often there has not been enough concern about the lack of professionalism and expertise on the part of those who visit the sick, bring communion, and anoint the sick.[39]

A 1995 publication from the NCCB, entitled *Ethical and Religious Directives for Catholic Health Care Services*,[40] was a welcome contribution that began to address the imbalance of the seeming one-sided enthusiasm for maintaining and growing the relationship between medicine and spirituality. Most notable was its honest admission that both the field of medicine and circumstances within the Church have changed dramatically.

> Health care in the United States is marked by extraordinary change. Not only is there continuing change in clinical practice due to technological advances, but the health care system in the United States is being challenged by both institutional and social factors as well. At the same time, there are a number of developments within the Catholic Church affecting the ecclesial mission of health care. Among these are significant changes in religious orders and congregations, the increased involvement of lay men and women, a heightened awareness of the Church's social role in the world, and developments in moral theology since the Second Vatican Council. A contemporary understanding of the Catholic health care ministry must take into account the new challenges presented by transitions both in the Church and in American society.[41]

The directives are primarily concerned with reaffirming "the ethical standards of behavior in health care that flow from the Church's teaching about the dignity of the human person" and second, to "provide authoritative guidance on certain moral issues that face Catholic healthcare today."[42] In spite of the reality that these aims are not the same as the many medical texts advocating a strengthening of the relationship between medicine and spirituality, there are some points of agreement between the two schools of writing.

> Through science the human race comes to understand God's wonderful work; and through technology it must conserve, protect, and perfect nature in harmony with God's purposes. Health care professionals pursue a special vocation to share in carrying forth God's life-

giving and healing work. The dialogue between medical science and Christian faith has for its primary purpose the common good of all human persons. It presupposes that science and faith do not contradict each other. Both are grounded in respect for truth and freedom. As new knowledge and new technologies expand, each person must form a correct conscience based on the moral norms for proper health care.[43]

It is in the third section, "The Professional–Patient Relationship," that some of the relational issues are finally addressed. The overall context is the primary relationship between the patient and the "professional health care provider[s]," consistent with the fact that it is often the case of a single patient and multiple specialists representing a team of providers. Without great elaboration there seems to be the same assumption that the physician (and others) will treat the whole person:

> The health care professional has the knowledge and experience to pursue the goals of healing, the maintenance of health, and the compassionate care of the dying, taking into account the patient's convictions and spiritual needs, and the moral responsibilities of all concerned. The person in need of health care depends on the skill of the health care provider to assist in preserving life and promoting health of body, mind, and spirit. The patient, in turn, has a responsibility to use these physical and mental resources in the service of moral and spiritual goals to the best of his or her ability.[44]

This summary statement regarding the relationship between the two fields builds on Part Two of the document, "The Pastoral and Spiritual Responsibility of Catholic Health Care," in which the pastoral care elements of patient care are addressed (such as listening, help in dealing with spiritual issues, and the administration of sacraments), but surprisingly the primary concern of team ministry is not between health professionals and ministers, but between parish ministers and the pastoral care department. "It is essential that there be very cordial and cooperative relationships between the personnel of pastoral care departments and the local clergy and ministers of care."[45] And again, "pastoral care personnel should work in close collaboration with local parishes and community clergy. Appropriate pastoral services and/or referrals should be available to all in keeping with their religious beliefs or affiliation."[46] The bulk of the chapter is taken up with differentiating what Catholic ministers themselves may do. "Priests, deacons, religious, and laity exercise diverse but complementary roles in this pastoral care,[47] with a number of directives describing particular situations and who may be involved. Not a single section or directive of the pastoral care specifics deals with the professional medical staff as cooperative team members along with the pastoral care providers. In this pivotal section it reads as though all the enthusiastic work for spirituality and striving towards healing the whole person within the field of medicine was unknown, or worse, considered irrelevant.

Certainly some authors in theology are aware of the shift in thinking toward spirituality in health care, often carefully acknowledging the growing distinction between " . . . the science of curing disease and the art of healing the patient's illness. In this sense, to *cure* is to treat diseased organs and tissues, looking not at the person but the pathology. On the other hand, to *heal* is to render patients at ease as whole persons within the structure of their spiritual worldview, their families, and their culture. Healing is largely about restoration that begins inside the patient."[48] While it is disappointing not to see this reflected in official Church documents, the 1995 document has given rise to subsequent local directives which address the necessary cooperative roles and the changed circumstances that both necessitate and enable that cooperation.

Why is this relationship between spirituality and medicine important for anointing of the sick? In the introduction to the PCS the theological rationale states "the sick person is not the only one who should fight against illness. Doctors and all who are devoted in any way to caring for the sick should consider it their duty to use all the means which in their judgment may help the sick, both physically and spiritually" (PCS 4). The cooperation with and through the primary giver of care, the physician, is a concrete way to facilitate healing. In a very direct way, the work of many professional health care workers in surveying and analyzing the benefits of religious faith and activity to understand how they benefit the patient is a direct embodiment of the theological directive in the PCS. If the fields of theology and medicine remain in competition with each other, as if in a turf war, what message is sent to the sick person who takes the Church's message of wholeness to heart?

Health care services, institutionally, socially, and technologically, will certainly continue to grow more complex in the near future, as will the lived experience of the patient in a pluralistic, multicultural, and multifaith world. These realities together mean that an insular approach to healing will be less and less pastoral, particularly when a large percentage of pastoral care of the sick takes place in hospitals that embody these pluralistic realities of modern life.

The intersection of professional health care and pastoral care of the sick is part of the conversation that must continue between the Church and the world. The Church's contextualization in a pluralistic world brings us to a related but separate conversation—the issue of popular United States culture and how it affects the reception and understanding of pastoral care of the sick, particularly the reception of the anointing of the sick by many people who are ill.

Pastoral Care of the Sick and Popular Religious Culture(s)

The matter proper for the sacrament is olive oil or, according to circumstances, other oil derived from plants (PCS 20).

Depending on the culture and traditions of different peoples, the number of anointings may be increased and the place of anointing may be changed. Directives on this should be included in the preparation of particular rituals (PCS 24).

In virtue of the Constitution on the Liturgy (art. 63b), the conferences of bishops have the right to prepare a section in particular rituals corresponding to the present section of the Roman Ritual and adapted to the needs of the different parts of the world. This section is for use in the regions concerned once the *acta* have been reviewed by the Apostolic See.

The following are the responsibilities of the conferences of bishop in this regard:

a. to decide on the adaptations dealt with in the Constitution on the Liturgy, article 39;

b. to weigh carefully and prudently what elements from the traditions and culture of individual peoples may be appropriately admitted into divine worship, then to propose to the Apostolic See adaptations considered useful or necessary that will be introduced with its consent;

c. to retain elements in the rites of the sick that now exist in particular rituals, as long as they are compatible with the Constitution on the Liturgy and with contemporary needs; or to adapt any of these elements;

d. to prepare translations of the texts so that they are truly adapted to the genius of different languages and cultures and to add, whenever appropriate, suitable melodies for singing;

e. to adapt and enlarge, if necessary, this Introduction in the Roman Ritual in order to encourage the conscious and active participation of the faithful;

f. to arrange the material in the editions of liturgical books prepared under the direction of the conferences of bishops in a format that will be as suitable as possible for pastoral use (PCS 38).

Whenever the Roman Ritual gives several alternative texts, particular rituals may add other texts of the same kind (PCS 39).

The minister should take into account the particular circumstances, needs, and desires of the sick and of other members of the faithful and should willingly use the various opportunities that the rites provide.

a. The minister should be especially aware that the sick tire easily and their physical condition may change from day to day and even from hour to hour. For this reason the celebration may be shortened if necessary.

b. When there is no group of the faithful present, the priest should remember that the Church is already present in his own person and in the one who is ill. For this reason he should try to offer the sick person the love and help of the Christian community both before and after the celebration of the sacrament. He may ask another Christian from the local community to do this if the sick person will accept this help.

c. Sick persons who regain their health after being anointed should be encouraged to give thanks for the favor received by participation in a Mass of thanksgiving or by some other suitable means (PCS 40).

The priest should follow the structure of the rite in the celebration, while accommodating it to the place and the people involved. The penitential rite may be part of the introductory rite or take place after the reading from Scripture. In place of the thanksgiving over the oil, the priest may give an instruction. This alternative should be considered when the sick person is in a hospital and other sick people present do not take part in the celebration of the sacrament (PCS 41).

As extensive as the official instructions on adaptation are, the reality is that the entire PCS is both sensitive and flexible in many different circumstances. This is truly liturgical inculturation, even if not the type of ethnic or linguistic differences often associated with the word itself.

All the sacramental actions of the Church exist only in culture, in the midst of communities that are culturally bound, and always through rites that are themselves the product of multiple historical cultures. The PCS is particularly sensitive to multicultural realities for two additional reasons. The first is that sickness and despair are not limited to Christians celebrating within the Christian community; as with weddings and funerals, all people marry, all people die, and in this case, all people get sick. From a Christian perspective, the rite addresses sickness and alienation as experiences shared by all humans, and the settings in which these rites are often celebrated are not always exclusively Christian, a factor which contributes to the pluralistic and sometimes ambiguous understandings of the rite's theology.

The second point is more specific to the rituals surrounding the sick, however, and brings us to the heart of a popular and widespread spirituality movement that is impacting many areas of "traditional" religion. The so-called "New Age" movement has, in many ways, become as mainstream as any institutional religion in the United States and spiritual healing is one of the unifying hallmarks linking the otherwise diverse beliefs and practices of the overall phenomenon of New Age practice.[49] The first reaction to associating New Age thinking with the anointing of the sick might be to assume that Eastern mysticism as a religion has very little to do with Catholic Christian sacraments. But the line between inculturation and syncretism with regard to certain practices became blurry enough to elicit a papal warning in a 1993 *ad limina* visit,[50] and a Vatican document in February 2003.[51] The latter document represents the spectrum of Christian responses to the New Age movement,[52] but recognizes in responsible ways the integrity of "the unquenchable longing of the human spirit for transcendence and religious meaning"[53] which has led to the tremendous success of elements of New Age spirituality.

> It has been said quite correctly that many people hover between certainty and uncertainty these days, particularly in questions relating to their identity. Some say that the Christian religion is patriarchal and authoritarian, that political institutions are unable to improve the world and that formal (allopathic) medicine simply fails to heal people effectively. The fact that what were once central elements in society are now perceived as untrustworthy or lacking in genuine authority has created a climate where people look inward, into themselves, for meaning and strength.[54]

It is important to understand why so many of the ideas and practices of New Age spirituality are appealing, especially to active Christians. The reasons fall into three categories. The first is described in the quote immediately above, that people are looking for something they have not found elsewhere: "New Age is attractive mainly because so much of what it offers meets hungers often left unsatisfied by the established institutions."[55] No less a writer than Pope John Paul II sent a warning to take the movement and its appeal seriously: "Pastors must honestly ask whether they have paid sufficient attention to the thirst of the human heart for the true 'living water,' which only Christ our Redeemer can give."[56] This search for meaning in one's life is often mediated through actions. One needs to do something in order to get meaning, hence the desire to learn the techniques of meditation, chanting, yoga, etc. As with so many of the practices grouped under the title "New Age," there is nothing wrong with any of these in and of themselves. It is only the exclusivity of these when understood or presented as the means to salvation that presents a contradictory theology to Christianity, an approach that was summarized as "Pelagian" by the Vatican study.[57]

A second category of appeal for the approach and understandings of New Age practices is its truly American inculturation: "New Age appeals to people imbued with the values of modern culture. Freedom, authenticity, self-reliance and the like are all held to be sacred. It appeals to those who have problems with patriarchy." It has been well accepted "because the world view on which it was based was already widely accepted. The ground was well prepared by the growth and spread of relativism, along with an antipathy or indifference toward the Christian faith."[58] While some of the rationale above seems confusing as to why it represents a problem, the Vatican document lists other issues that perhaps resonate better with contemporary Christians. One is what the study describes as two particular appeals to Catholics: "psychological affirmation of the individual" and "increasing nostalgia and curiosity for the wisdom and ritual of long ago."[59] Another is the increasing global polarization between fundamentalism on the one hand and a desire to be totally inclusive on the other. Total inclusivity can result, according to its critics, in blindly accepting all religions as equally relevant and true, or at least in dissolving any real or imagined differences in a "syncretism of esoteric and secular elements."[60] This harmony or blending of world religions into one is often stated as a goal of New Age proponents.[61]

The third category of appeal of New Age spirituality is that those drawn towards it have tried traditional Christianity or other faiths and have found them lacking, parallel to a disillusion with secular institutions. The perceived lack of attention to the individual, a cultural stumbling block to a religious system such as Christianity,[62] and the divergence between culturally driven ideals and the often unarticulated goals of the Christian life seem to be the generic bases for differences.

> Basically, the appeal of the New Age has to do with the culturally stimulated interest in the self, its value, capacities and problems. Whereas traditionalized religiosity, with its hierarchical organization, is well suited for the community, detraditionalized spirituality is well suited for the individual. The New Age is "of" the self in that it facilitates celebration of what it is to be and to become; and "for" the self in that by differing from much of the mainstream, it is positioned to handle identity problems generated by conventional forms of life.[63]

The oddly joined goals of many New Age programs—"countercultural values with the mainstream need to succeed, inner satisfaction with outer success"[64]—are not limited to middle-class North America. On a global scale and even within "third world" countries, there are descriptions of Latin American Protestant church movements and traditional African churches where "people today are looking for solutions, not for eternity."[65] This desire for a type of spiritual quick fix is augmented by a widespread and very real sense of alienation and a lack of trust in institutions, or at least a distrust in institutional abilities to address the immediate problems in peoples' lives.

There are a variety of new cultural forces at play. When these factors—hunger for meaning in life and the desire to bring that meaning about, cultural pressures to be both spiritually and materially successful, and disillusionment with religious and secular institutions—are brought to bear on sickness and health, the result has and will continue to impact the understanding and doing of the rituals in PCS. The most obvious point of alignment between New Age emphases and the contemporary rite is the centrality and desirability of wholeness.

The secondary writings about anointing of the sick often stress the goal of wholeness as both a fundamental effect of the sacrament and as a primary means of distinguishing between healing and cure.[66] If substantial, tangible, and obvious physical healing (the most discernable type of healing to note) does not come about as a result of the anointing, then another type of healing must be occurring, and this is often described in terms of wholeness (wholeness within the individual, between the individual and his/her community, between the individual and God), or overcoming alienation on many levels. Implicit in both New Age teachings and in the stress on wholeness in the PCS is the overcoming of any lingering dualism. While much New Age writing implies that Christianity (or the Judeo-Christian tradition) is the source for this dualism, throughout its history Christianity itself has had to fight against internal heterodox emphases on spirit-matter dualism in particular. A ritual manifestation of this mutual striving toward wholeness and overcoming dualism is the stress on the importance of the body and its essential cooperation with the mind in the healing process. While the rite of anointing itself certainly addresses the physical concerns of the sick and suffering, the extension of the emphasis is clearly coming from external sources. One ritual extension that is increasingly common in many urban centers is the practice of massage with oils. The importance of touch as a contribution to healing is widely discussed, although confirmed more through anecdotal rather than scientific survey. Increasingly the use of massage therapy, chaplains trained in modified massage or family members touching and rubbing with herbal oils, serves as a follow-up to the sacrament of the anointing of the sick, or as a substitute for it in places where no priest is available to attend to the ill person. Ancillary ritual practices may include body therapies such as reflexology and orgonomy, music therapy, and the use of meditation practices and devices (such as meditation bowls) from different Buddhist traditions.

How does familiarity with these practices, and in many cases, engagement with these practices, affect the reception by practicing Catholic Christians of the rituals associated with PCS? Acceptance of a wide spectrum of ritual action is reflected in the integration of extra rituals into the anointing of the sick, often in cases where family members are fully engaged and interested in participation or in larger communal celebrations of the rite. Many of the practices have long-standing Christian roots, although they are more familiar to many contemporary Americans in their non-Christian presentations. And many of these practices are not limited to clergy, or have no presumptions of clerical exclusivity, falling into the category of popular religious practices not requiring the services of the spiritual professional. Why are these practices increasingly popular? Why are the expansive and flexible rites of the Church perceived by many to be not enough? It seems that at the root it is not so much a matter of being able to actively participate or not, but rather that the rites do not seem to "work" and that family and friends feel a desire and an obligation to try everything they can to help the sick individual at the center of the care and concern. Nowhere is this more apparent than in a number of immigrant communities in which there is a cultural tradition of physical healing as well as a renewed enthusiasm for seeing the ministry of Jesus' healing as rightfully that of the Church. Some have explained the phenomenon as a Christianization of an indigenous healing tradition:

> If we find that Africa's flourishing indigenous churches place a far greater weight on healing than do their Northern neighbors, we might be tempted to explain this in terms of the functions expected of religion in traditional African society. On the other hand, spiritual healing has frequently characterized new and fringe religious movements in Europe and North America over the centuries, and the theme might be seen as a universal element in popular religion.[67]

But this flourishing does not occur in "fringe" communities alone. One of the most prominent figures arguing for the centrality of physical healing in the Church has been an African archbishop, Emmanuel Milingo. In spite of his notoriety for other issues, Milingo epitomized the perspective of African Christians at home and abroad by placing "spiritual healing and exorcism at the center of his ministry, combining traditional beliefs with the language of the charismatic revival."[68] Similar emphases have emerged (or have finally been noticed) throughout Latin America,[69] and American based immigrants have brought these concerns and expectations with them.

The rites of the Church do not seem to produce the right results for many people, and the medical world, with all its promise of infallibility, also fails the sick in their eyes.

> Science and technology have clearly failed to deliver all they once seemed to promise, so in their search for meaning and liberation people have turned to the spiritual realm. New Age as we now know it came from a search for something more humane and beautiful than the oppressive, alienating experience of life in Western society.[70]

For a number of people, the crushing realization that medical cures for worldwide epidemics have thus far proved elusive has ended the sense that everything can be medically "fixed." When joined to the reality that we are, to a certain extent, individually responsible for much preventative care for good health (diet, exercise, lifestyle choices), it invites the expectation that we can complement, compete, or augment the medical regime with various spiritual practices, thus achieving the desired results.

While the rites of the Church, such as anointing the sick, make no promises of physical healing, the popular spirituality and religiosity of the culture around the celebration of the rites seems to suggest that it should promise physical healing.

This sense that we should be able to solve the problem of sickness either through technology or through ritual manifests a point of contention between New Age popular beliefs and the rites of the sick. In the previous chapter the relationship between sin and sickness was discussed. There we heard the strong statement of the *praenotanda* disavowing any direct cause-and-effect relationship between personal sin and sickness (PCS 2). The precise relationship between sin and sickness in the rite, however, is not defined. That there is a relationship between sin and sickness is made clear in the sacramental focus on both, and the extensive discussions in secondary literature often characterize the relationship as an issue of wholeness. If the whole person is to be healed, issues of physical health, emotional health, mental health, and spiritual health (sin) need to be taken into consideration and addressed. Because we are psychosomatic beings, our break in relationship with God or with our neighbor is bound to affect our relationship with our own bodies. At first glance, this type of approach seems to have little to do with New Age sympathies where sin is not considered a helpful or appropriate concept.

> In New Age there is no distinction between good and evil. Human actions are the fruit of either illumination or ignorance. Hence we cannot condemn anyone, and nobody needs forgiveness. Believing in the existence of evil can create only negativity and fear.[71]

The cultural influences of New Age do contribute to American Christian views by helping to convey the sense that we should be able to affect our own health and wholeness through our actions. In much New Age thinking, "illness and suffering come from working against nature; when one is in tune with nature, one can expect a much healthier life and even material prosperity."[72] The implication is that if we are sick it is because of something we have done, or not done. Therefore, if we could just be in harmony with the world, our neighbors, our family, and our God, the sickness should go away. This type of inculturation is really a syncretism inasmuch as it denies the wisdom and will of God in the course of human affairs. The all-too-common fear, even among faithful Christians, that personal sin has caused sickness (or that it is specifically a punishment from God) does not need additional confirmation from an inculturated assumption that we bring sickness upon ourselves because we are not appropriately in balance with all living things. If we are ultimately responsible for our own health, if the "source of healing is said to be within ourselves,"[73] then when sickness comes for reasons quite other than personal actions, it can lead only to hopelessness and despair. Throughout the PCS an important antidote to this sole dependence on oneself for both health and happiness is the articulation of an "authentic spirituality" that is "not so much our search for God, but God's search of us."[74]

As with all true liturgical inculturation, both the culture and the liturgical rite will be changed by the encounter between Christianity and New Age practices.[75] Perhaps what some American Catholics can benefit from is the cultural impact of personal responsibility for many aspects of health as well as encouragement to participate actively in exercising one's spiritual muscles. By extension the Church as a whole can recommit itself to the importance of catechesis. The Vatican study concluded that much of the confusion was a result of a weakness in understanding the core content, or fundamentals, of Christian faith.[76] And a contribution to the larger culture from the rites of and for the sick is that there is Someone beyond ourselves to whom we can turn when the unexplainable happens, that hopelessness and despair are not the inevitable results of serious sickness, and that we do not, ultimately, need to save ourselves.

Human Suffering and Pastoral Care of the Sick

Suffering and illness have always been among the greatest problems that trouble the human spirit. Christians feel and experience pain as do all other people; yet their faith helps them to grasp more deeply the mystery of suffering and to bear their pain with greater courage. From Christ's words they know that sickness has meaning and value for their own salvation and for the salvation of the world (PCS 1).

Christ himself, who is without sin, in fulfilling the words of Isaiah took on all the wounds of his passion and shared in all human pain. Christ is still pained and tormented in his members, made like him. Still, our afflictions seem but momentary and slight when compared to the greatness of the eternal glory for which they prepare us (PCS 2).

> We should always be prepared to fill up what is lacking in Christ's sufferings for the salvation of the world as we look forward to creation's being set free in the glory of the children of God. (PCS 3)

> This sacrament gives the grace of the Holy Spirit to those who are sick . . . Thus the sick person is able not only to bear suffering bravely, but also to fight against it. (PCS 6)

If God is all-powerful and all-good, why is there suffering in the world? Why especially do faithful Christians suffer? These are certainly not new questions; they have formed the core of religious reflection for as long as human beings have recorded their engagement with the questions of who God is and who we are in relation to God. But human experience expands, and, in that expansion, theology must also expand and respond by bringing the core of tradition forward to meet new formative contexts.

The experience of suffering on a mass scale, such as through war or natural disasters, can lead to a sense of utter hopelessness and the conviction that God is nowhere to be found. Coupled with the modern ability to access information on disasters throughout the world almost as they happen leads inevitably to an overwhelming sense of failure when trying to cope with the information mentally and emotionally. On an individual level, the personal experience of pain, whether physical or other, can be the defining moment of faith. But it is often only after the shock of experiencing an intimate and unwanted reality in a world accustomed to virtual detachment that the reality of pain sinks in. Physical pain is not, however, the sum total of personal suffering.

> Suffering is more than pain. There is psychic and moral suffering, suffering from loneliness and from the conscious experience of decay. Along with this suffering and all sorts of other pain, there is the question of meaning, the struggle with senselessness. By day patients ask "I have headaches, can I have a pill?", but by night "I have headaches, what did I do to deserve this?" The night's questions ask why.[77]

The inevitable sense that one has done something to deserve this suffering, and then trying to reconcile that with one's image of God can lead either to growth and insight or further alienation and bitterness.

These scenarios exemplify the breadth of the scope of writing concerned with the theology of suffering and of theodicy (the "justification of God in the light of evil and suffering"),[78] covering a spectrum from corporate evil and social suffering on one end to individual suffering through physical, psychological, emotional, or spiritual pain on the other. For our purposes we will limit our study to the dimensions of suffering that impact individual Christians who are the focus of the anointing of the sick, along with their families and friends who surround them in times of sickness and suffering, specifically as the dimensions of suffering are raised through the rite itself and its theological introduction.

The perception of many people outside the Church (as well as some within the Church) is that the Church's care for the sick is crystallized in its reaction to and articulation of the suffering endured by individuals. Out of the two contexts explored above in this chapter, the world of medicine and the popular religiosity of American culture, come particular challenges, both theoretical and physical, to the reality of suffering. The health profession has made tremendous strides in alleviating physical suffering, primarily through new and stronger medications and better surgical procedures. The challenge remains to eradicate all physical pain, which is the primary definition of suffering. But pain is not seen as a moral evil from the perspective of the health care profession. Pain first has a positive role in that it "can function as an alarm, a warning signal that we are somehow being threatened. Were it not for the experience of pain, the threat to our well-being might go unnoticed,"[79] as with our reflective move away from fire. After this initial usefulness of pain, however, chronic pain is no longer necessary in signaling an alarm or in assisting in a medical diagnosis and can therefore be safely removed by some type of medical intervention. But when the physical pain cannot be removed, in spite of the advanced technological skills of physicians and others, the limits of modern medicine become all too readily apparent to those involved. The challenge to the Church and its rites for the sick is first to take a stand on suffering, to acknowledge it as something to be struggled against, and then to imbue it with meaning. "Pain demands a response, while suffering demands an interpretation."[80]

The popular cultural views on suffering and pain, captured in some of the discussion on the New Age movement above, often stem from information overload. Our culture might be characterized as simply numb, what Robert Lifton calls "psychic numbing."[81] Others attribute it to more insidious cultural traits: "every culture has its own specific pathology; ours has been described as narcissism. The narcissistic personality is characterized by its inability to recognize how others feel; pathological narcissists suffer from apathy."[82] But certainly individualism, "greed as creed" consumerism, and contemporary politics contribute to this inability to discern a reality beyond oneself or away from the primary focus on acquisition more than the New Age focus on self-fulfillment and self-reliance. In whatever way these factors contribute to the lack of empathy or engagement, the consensus from a number of theologians is that "our contemporary culture is characterized by its overwhelming attempt to eliminate negativity; it is marked by the repression of pain and the consequent incapacity to suffer; it fosters the incapacity to confront and appropriate the reality of suffering."[83] The challenge to the Church in its pastoral care of the sick, then, is to articulate the reality and the experience of suffering, to assure the suffering individual (and their circles of community) that suffering has meaning, and to articulate a Christian interpretation of the meaning of suffering through the relationship between the suffering of Christ and that of the individual Christian. Therefore, it becomes a primary task of the Church not only to say that suffering and community are real for both the sake of speaking the truth and for the sake of comfort and solidarity with the suffering, but to articulate what and how suffering means and what it does for the individual, for the Church, and for the world.

The acknowledgment of the presence of suffering is the first and therefore primary motif of the General Introduction ("suffering and illness have always been among the greatest problems that trouble the human spirit" [PCS 1]). The first three paragraphs deal with suffering, and by framing the interpretive introduction in a context of suffering, the reality is both acknowledged and confronted. The rite of anointing of the sick itself, however, seems to presume that acknowledging the reality of suffering will be incorporated into the adaptable elements spoken by the priest,[84] the formal prayers of the rite mention suffering only in other specific contexts. Particularly in the beginning of the rite (the greeting and various options for the instruction) the flexibility invites the concrete circumstances of the sick to be acknowledged.

> In this Ritual it is not possible to provide a ready made introduction (that is, by the minister) because the circumstances always vary. Is this not the case for many of the texts as well? Indeed during the whole celebration one may not pass over what people in fact are experiencing. To this end the liturgical text strives to create an atmosphere in which the sick and all those present can express, or can hear expressed, their pain, anxiety and questions, their hopelessness, despair and anger, as well as their hope and expectations. They can reach out to God: "Where are you? What is your purpose in all of this?" To this end the Ritual offers a number of appropriate alternate texts.[85]

The great advantage of the rites for the sick, and especially the anointing of the sick, is the flexibility that allows engagement of people in many different places, but that flexibility is also its great danger; the choices must be made wisely with a sense of where the patient is, not just medically, but particularly in their understanding and view of suffering and of God.

After the counter-cultural acknowledgment that suffering exists, the rite and its theological explanation must also counter the recurring view that the Church somehow believes suffering is desirable. There have been times and movements in the history of the Church when the paradox of fighting against suffering and accepting uncontrollable suffering has not been presented or understood as a sequential tension, or even as a paradox at all. Suffering is not a Christian goal. *Good*

> If human suffering is accepted as something necessary, it is a relatively small step to the actual seeking after some form of suffering . . . Culturally, we can refer to a certain kind of "dolorism," a type of spiritual masochism that presumes that suffering is something good, something that can be beneficial or even rewarding . . . Carried to its extreme, such an ideology . . . evolves into a cult, something sought after for its own sake. It inspires a masochistic spirituality that not only results in the stagnation of human development; it also opens the possibility of manipulation and oppression.[86]

In paragraph six of the General Introduction, the effects of the sacrament as listed include the ability to "not only bear suffering bravely, but also to fight against it." Prior to that, the eye is drawn to paragraph three where, after being urged to fight "strenuously against all sickness and carefully seek the blessings of good health," we are reminded that "we should always be prepared to fill up what is lacking in Christ's sufferings for the salvation of the world." The Christian paradox of suffering is thus presented; it is to be fought against strenuously, but when it is unavoidable, it is to be interpreted as having distinctive Christian meanings. But, while these two perspectives are kept in necessary tension in the doctrinal texts, the reality of accepting suffering and the obligation to struggle against it are virtually absent from the liturgical texts.

The concept of suffering is present in several of the prayers throughout the three forms of anointing of the sick (individual, communal, abbreviated for hospital/institution), but the dominant interpretive context is relief from suffering. This context of solidarity and comfort is an important one for the pastoral care of the sick, not only for the direct comfort of the sick individual and his or her family and friends, but also as an active counter-cultural demonstration against delusions of autonomy and self-control. If a major focus of the sacrament is to overcome the levels of alienation (from oneself, from one's communities, and from one's God), then the countering of suffering by the comforting presence of the triune God and through the solidarity of the caring community, whose very presence is representative of the Church and God,[87] is an important facet of the grace of wholeness and inclusion. In the American translation, however, the explicit expression of solidarity (for the sick) is not as clear as in the Flemish and French texts, replaced as it is by the emphasis on alleviation of suffering. "Relieve the suffering of all the sick [here present]" (Litany, PCS 121); "God of mercy, ease the sufferings and comfort the weakness of your servant" (Thanksgiving over Blessed Oil, PCS 123); "Grant N. comfort in her suffering" (Prayer after Anointing, PCS 125); and in multiple choices of Scripture readings presented in the appendix (Part III, PCS 297).

In addition, the importance of human forgiveness and reconciliation in the easing of psychological, emotional, and spiritual suffering are not present in the rite. There is both an allowance for the sacrament of reconciliation and for a penitential rite in the anointing of the sick, but the penitential rite does not allow for the mutual forgiveness that sometimes needs to be spoken between the seriously ill person and family and friends present at the rite. The addition of this would be a concrete response to the repeated preference for the rite to be done in the midst of the gathered Church, as sign and symbol of the solidarity of the community and the sick person, as well as sign of the love of God.[88]

Finally, with regard to suffering and its explication in both the doctrinal and liturgical texts of the rite, the most expansive theology is that dealing with meaning. How and why does suffering mean in the Christian context? And if it means something, what does it mean? And what does human suffering say of God? Human beings are certainly cognizant of different kinds of suffering and of different sources of suffering. Some suffering can at least be partially comprehended because it has a discernable cause, such as the suffering caused by criminal actions or war. "In such cases, human agency has played at least a collaborative role; God does not have to be directly responsible for the suffering perpetrated through human sinfulness."[89] But the unexplainable, the suffering of innocent children, natural disasters, and other catastrophes leave one wondering how God could have allowed this. Perhaps the primary question brought to theology is the incomprehensibility of meaningless suffering, what Schillebeeckx calls the "basic human question."[90] And the seemingly simple question gives rise to complex answers. Whether one intellectualizes the issue inclusively (the inclusive model presumes that "suffering, in one way or another, is the will of God"), where suffering functions as a means to an end, leading to a determinism, or exclusively leading to a future solution or indeterminism (the exclusive model assumes that "suffering is not directly the will of God"),[91] the relationship between a theology or articulation of suffering and what it says of God is unavoidable. The rite itself introduces its entry into theodicy by saying that suffering is a mystery grasped "more deeply" because of faith (PCS 1). In the theological understanding of mystery, then, suffering both reveals and conceals divine wisdom, remaining both revelatory and hidden in itself and toward that to which it points.

Qualitatively and quantitatively it is the christological associations of suffering that demand one's attention throughout the rite. Part of the mystery of the christic meanings associated with suffering is its very eschatological framework; suffering exists between what has been accomplished once and for all ("In the splendor of his rising your Son conquered suffering and death" [Eucharistic Prayer, PCS 145]; "by your paschal mystery you have won for us salvation" [Penitential Rite, PCS 118C]) and what will be ("as these gifts . . . will be transformed into the risen Lord, so may he unite our sufferings with his and cause us to rise to new life" [Prayer over the Gifts, PCS 144A]; "May God fill your heart with peace and lead you to eternal life" [Blessing, PCS 147A]).

One of the more perplexing associations of suffering imbued with christological meaning is in PCS 3: "We should always be prepared to fill up what is lacking in Christ's sufferings for the salvation of the world." The biblical references refer first to Colossians 1:24 and secondly to Romans 8:19-21. In English the paragraph almost reads as though there is an implication of something missing or inadequate in Christ's suffering and death, certainly a misunderstanding in both the broader spectrum of systematic theology and within the apostle Paul's own theology and writings. But the NRSV and other translations of the key Colossians verse "offer a widespread mistranslation of 1:24b, which has given rise to a series of false promises."[92] Rather than the frequently heard ". . . and in my flesh I am completing what is lacking in Christ's afflictions for the sake of his body, that is, the church," several biblical commentators argue that the verse should read (or be understood to read) "I complete what is lacking in the sufferings-of-Christ-in-my-flesh"[93] or "I complete what is needed of the Christian sufferings in my flesh for his body."[94] Both translations try to go beyond the broadest spectrum of translation possibilities[95] by drawing on linguistics and systematic Pauline theology. The point of most of the serious commentaries on the verse and its openness to mis-understanding is that it is not a direct reference to the historical Jesus or the individual Christ. Part of the hermeneutical key is to see the verse in relation to the servant passages in Isaiah, where there is

> an alternation between the servant as an individual and the servant as a corporate personality. In other words, Christ is still suffering through the sufferings of His people. What Paul endures is therefore an extension of the sufferings of Christ. These sufferings are on behalf of the body, the church as a whole, not just the local community.[96]

What the theological introduction to the pastoral care of the sick is calling its participants to, then, is the assurance, not only that when unavoidable suffering comes the suffering has meaning and purpose, but that Christ will join it to his own suffering as the whole body of Christ strives towards union in the resurrection. This primary meaning of suffering, that it has a purpose and is joined to the suffering of the ongoing body of Christ, has a long tradition of ritual association in Christian history. Most notably one thinks of the tradition dating from late antiquity of reading the Gospel passion accounts at the bedside of a dying Christian, weaving the two narratives together in a manifestation of the apostle Paul's writing to the Romans: "For if we have been united with him in a death like his, we will certainly be united with him in a resurrection like his" (Rom 6:5).[97] In addition, it is the language associated with hagiography, particularly with the martyr passions of the early Church, in which the sufferings of the martyrs were virtually subsumed into that of Christ, enabling them to endure without renouncing their faith.[98] Within the liturgical language of the rite itself the imagery of Christ sharing in the suffering of the individual Christian appears in varied places: "You renew among us now the wonders of your passion" (Penitential Rite, PCS 118C); "Since you have given him a share in your own passion, help him to find hope in suffering" (Prayer after Anointing for extreme or terminal illness, PCS 125C); "May all who share in his [Christ's] suffering find in these sacraments a source of fresh courage and healing" (Opening Prayer, PCS 136).

In spite of the role that human suffering plays as the "intermediary factor between the historical Jesus and his universal significance"[99] a distinction is maintained between the suffering of Christ and that of an individual Christian. "Christ himself, who is without sin, in fulfilling the words of Isaiah took on all the wounds of his passion and shared in all human pain. Christ is still pained and tormented in his members, made like him. Still, our afflictions seem but momentary and slight when compared to the greatness of the eternal glory for which they prepare us" (PCS 2). Here is another point of caution in the rite that requires the one making the choices of texts to choose wisely. Certainly the suffering of Christ for the redemption of the world is of a different magnitude than all other human suffering, but too passive an interpretation can project an image that may not acknowledge the very real suffering of the seriously sick individual.

> Human suffering is trivialized because of its relative insignificance in comparison with the so much greater, so much more intense, and so much more meaningful suffering of Christ—which takes away the sins of the world. Simultaneously, the operative image of God in this interpretation is a God who is almost exclusively transcendent, who is beyond any identification with human suffering.[100]

The liturgical texts of the rite do acknowledge the suffering of the individual when they ask for comfort and relief, but beyond those texts the integrity of the anointing of the sick requires a carefully thought out approach to articulating the relationship between the suffering of Christ in and through the body of Christ and the individual who is sick, particularly when his or her suffering is acute.

The reality of suffering and how it is addressed in the sacrament of anointing of the sick calls for reflection on the question of what suffering accomplishes. What is its effect? The heart of the rite's contribution to this aspect of the theology of suffering comes from the key paragraphs of the rite's *praenotanda*: "From Christ's own words they know that sickness has meaning and value for their own salvation and for the salvation of the world" (PCS 1), and "we should always be prepared to fill up what is lacking in Christ's sufferings for the salvation of the world as we look forward to creation's being set free in the glory of the children of God" (PCS 3). In addition, there is a striking statement in the Vatican II document on the Church *(Lumen Gentium)* which is quoted in paragraph five of the general introduction: the Church "exhorts [the sick] to contribute to the welfare of the People of God by freely uniting themselves to the passion and death of Christ."[101]

As with the contrast experience distinguishing between the suffering of Christ and the suffering of Christians, here also the key seems to be in a contrast, but one between what is now and what will be. In all three dimensions of salvific effect (for the individual level, for the Church, and for the world) there is an eschatological thrust in both the moral and ritual interpretations. Rather than the passive approach to suffering which skews both the intensity and reality of the suffering and the engagement of God,[102] an active approach allows the suffering person both to be and to articulate the contrast between the "already" and the "not yet." It also helps answer the question of how the sick minister to us as sign and symbol ("By their witness the sick show that our mortal life must be redeemed through the mystery of Christ's death and resurrection" [PCS 3]).

> When suffering is exposed as a form of relievable pain, we encounter the dynamics of the faith perspective in terms of its (radical) witness for the need to realize the best human possibility: its option for the poor and the weak, its call for reconciliation, and its (eschatological) hope in transforming the possible into the real. With respect to suffering that is genuinely understood to be non-relievable, tragic, and without evident meaning, a negative experience which lies beyond the capability of moral response, the role of faith is to assist in a process of clarification that neither trivializes the moral reflection nor reduces the meaning of the human experience of suffering through proposing a mere explanatory justification.[103]

The Flemish translation articulates this in clearer language than the U.S. rite:

> Continue to believe that your old age, your illness, your suffering has value for the church, and contributes to the building up of the community; that your suffering, like that of the Lord, can be a source of power and comfort for the sick and the healthy.[104]

In other words, one of the primary salvific effects of suffering, when it is "non-relievable," is in this witness and inspiration to those gathered around the sick individual. Schillebeeckx would go one step further and say that "suffering is not redemptive in itself, but it is redemptive when it is suffering through and for others . . . ."[105] The conscious faith-response to the love and presence of God through pastoral care and particularly through the sacrament of the anointing is to unite one's suffering to Christ's for the sake of the Church and of the world. This is the love that enables suffering to fulfill a functional role between the historical Jesus and the universal Christ.[106] "Our own experience of suffering on behalf of others is an authentic imitation of Jesus, 'an active *memoria passionis* of the Risen Lord.'"[107] The articulation of the active role in the rite also maintains a necessary tension between struggle and acceptance that prevents any illusion that suffering is somehow desirable or justified when preventable. In this way the "mystery of suffering" as the "mystery of salvation" presented in the general introduction is maintained both as realized eschatology and as a faith expression in the future.

Finally a critique of the contemporary rite of anointing of the sick related to the suffering of the sick seems necessary to mention. One of the effective ways of creating and expressing the relationship between the suffering of Christ and that of the individual is through narrative. If narrative is a way to construct the world, then to be able to see the context of their own suffering in their life stories is a way to make sense of suffering and its potential accomplishments for suffering and faithful Christians. In the rite for anointing of the sick, the narrative of Christ's suffering is presented in Scripture readings and in liturgical texts. But, in spite of the rite's ability to be adapted to various circumstances, one of the frequent complaints of those engaged in the liturgy (particularly as "recipients" of the anointing) is the lack of ritual space to weave their own fears, thoughts, and hopes into the ritual sequence. All sacramental acts make a double demand on the presider in that the one leading has to use both ritual skills, requiring a necessary detachment and distance in order to engage everyone present in a semblance of equality, and as well as personal, pastoral skills, requiring an intimacy and comfort level with one-on-one engagement.[108] One cannot hide behind a book in order to anoint the sick, nor can one make the entire rite a spontaneous, affective prayer. One must both preside and engage in touch and gesture, often alternating quickly between very different skills normatively present in different personality types. In a similar manner, the rite itself would benefit from a clearer invitation to both the comforting and engaging formality of structured and repetitive language and to dedicated space for honest conversation and emotion, very much like the best of face-to-face reconciliation rites. While this is secondary to the more important dimensions of human suffering, the opportunity to receive and give forgiveness, to verbally relate one's own narrative to that of Christ's, and to give thanks when "healed to life"[109] (PCS 40C), may contribute to wholeness and health for suffering individuals and all who care for them.

Pastoral Care of the Dying

This book has been a study of the pastoral care of the sick, but it may be beneficial to conclude with a reminder that the full title of the array of rituals and texts is *Pastoral Care of the Sick: Rites of Anointing and Viaticum*. In other words, the title itself calls our attention to two primary sacramental moments: anointing of the sick for the seriously sick and Viaticum for the dying. The sequence of rites moves through visiting the sick, communion, and anointing to Viaticum, commendation of the dying and prayers for the dead, without presuming that the former always implies the latter. But, the rite also does not deny that serious sickness is both a reminder of our own mortality and may indeed lead to death.

In the revisions of the rite for anointing the sick and its deliberate move away from extreme unction, a great deal of energy was expended on designing language that would remove any association with the last rites. In many cultures and geographical experiences of the anointing of the sick, this has been a very successful and dramatic change in the history of the sacrament. But as with any sacramental rite that is experienced as a reality in the lives of people, some criticism has crept in regarding the disassociation of the rite from that of dying.

> Since Vatican Council II emphasis has been placed on the idea that the anointing of the sick is no longer (or no longer primarily) the sacrament of the dying, but of the seriously ill. Does this imply that death is passed over in silence, or that we ignore the seriousness of the situation? The Ritual, or at least the way in which some have celebrated the sacrament, has been criticized on this account. But does not every serious illness make us conscious of the death that, sooner or later, we must undergo? Certainly the whole Ritual, and the anointing of the sick as well, directs our attention to our final destination.[110]

The tension between reserving the anointing of the sick for those who are seriously sick and those who would encourage a more general and repeatable use of the rite has already been discussed in an earlier chapter. And, while not all would agree that the rite needs to literally address death in every instance, there is an almost studied avoidance of death in many celebrations that seems to have a great affinity with the cultural inability to talk about or deal with death.[111] But the point here is not the presence or absence of that literal connection in the rite, but rather a tentative suggestion to consider expanding the official circumstances of anointing of the sick to include the dying. The practice of anointing the dying is certainly present in many hospitals and institutions, documented through anecdotes and statistics,[112] but aside from various occasional voices calling for a return to extreme unction,[113] it is not part of any official theological discussion. Viaticum remains, rightly, the primary sacrament for the dying. But there are newer considerations arising from the interplay between medical technology and culture that beg the question be raised again.

One is the theoretical question of what some scholars perceive as an anthropological question (although one with its origins in the practical and pastoral world of palliative care). Kristiaan Depoortere asks:

> Has the Vatican II view of the anointing of the sick taken sufficient account of all kinds of anthropological demands? Doesn't the stubborn association of anointing and dying mean that the sick want to reserve that gesture for the last moment?[114]

He bases his observations on pastoral experience in the breakdown with all three of the suggested sacraments for the sick. First, the sacrament of reconciliation, he says, "is undergoing a severe crisis in the West. Even many practicing Catholics no longer ever make a personal confession." Secondly, he has observed that the anointing, often celebrated "when there is no danger to life . . . succeeds in avoiding a personal confrontation with mortality." But he believes that faithful people do want more, and feels that they "are asking vitally and viscerally for a rite of transition, certainly for the last passage. Too early an anointing robs them of this. People do not want to be anointed unless they themselves—or their families—really feel that it is now or never." Finally, the third sacrament, Viaticum, succeeds theologically from his perspective, "the best is saved for last, namely food for the way to the other side." But its very success is perhaps its downfall. "In our Christian hospitals many believers communicate twice a week. So at an anthropological level the supreme sacrament does not work as a ritual of transition."[115] Depoortere does not argue for a return to extreme unction but for a serious reflection on the "growing dissociation between faith and healing" with its ramifications for the forgiveness of sins and understandings of sacramental grace in general.[116]

It is his final, unexplored comment in the article that I found the most compelling and consonant with personal experience. He mentions very briefly the "many medical and practical problems around communion for the dying."[117] The reality of dying for many people in this country, faithful Christians themselves and/or surrounded by faithful (and fearful) friends and family, is an extended one since those dying are usually attached to an array of life support apparatus. The actual moment of death is often difficult to discern, coming hours after the life support has been removed as a result of a medical decision that its continuation is beyond extraordinary support or hope for recovery. There is no opportunity for communion under either species in these cases, but only touch, prayer, and blessing, and commendation when timely. But the faithful and fearful gathered around the patient, and perhaps the patient him- or herself whose cognizance is often underestimated,[118] understandably want something to be done. Whether the ritual action is understood to contribute to the salvation of the individual or whether it is actually for the comfort and assurance of the mourners, there is a great need and a great pressure to do something. It is this desire for "something" that often leads to creative and unofficial actions by lay ministers and chaplains, but many of the stories of prayers and anointing are from family members themselves. This type of situation, increasing in number and location, seems like an invitation to consider an extraordinary rite of anointing when all other substantial rituals of transition are not possible.

These are realities beyond the scope of the original authors of the Pastoral Care of the Sick. But liturgy does not exist in a vacuum and changing circumstances call either for a restatement of the established ritual or appropriate adaptations where necessary. All of the challenges—medical, cultural, theological, or anthropological—raise far more questions than answers. Where are medical technology and our cultural assumptions leading the rite in the twenty-first century?[119] Are medical changes surrounding the way we die an invitation to reconsider an anointing for the dying with appropriate texts and rituals?

Conclusion

This chapter has concerned itself with issues on the boundaries of the rites for the sick, but particularly as those issues pertain to the sacramental heart of the order, the Anointing of the Sick. The rite itself has valuable lessons to teach regarding a theological understanding of human suffering. The scope of the theology in at least the doctrinal sections of the rite seems barely tapped as far as their potential for fruitful catechesis and, more importantly, for the comfort and support of those individuals in acute pain and suffering.

For different reasons, the relationship of the health care profession to the world of spirituality as summarized in liturgical rite is a hopeful sign. The contemporary openness to seeing more than meets the eye, to embracing a spiritual reality and a divine power alive and active in our world suggests we may be on the edge of a breakthrough, and the medical profession, long opposed to any collaborative discussion, seems open to greater dialogue. The official ecclesial recognition of changes within the health care profession and startling changes within the way the Church ministers to its sick and suffering has been slower, but appears to be most fruitful at the grassroots level, often in the form of local and diocesan presentations and concerns. The continuing cooperative relationship and opening to mutual respect can only serve to benefit the sick individuals who are the focus of both the Church's pastoral care and health professionals' attention.

Less clear is the relationship between the Church's ministry to the sick and the widespread interest in spiritual healing. In many instances, the relationship seems a fruitful inculturation, encouraging active Christians to participate not in other, but in more, ways. The return to meditation, contemplative practices, ritual, and prayer seems a path to what is good and desirable. The insidious, as yet undiscerned, side is how the two perspectives, Christian, and, for lack of a better term, "New Age," make adjustments when their similar practices arise from very different theologies. Where is the line between inculturation and syncretism? Is it really as major a concern as the Vatican teaching hints at, challenging and misleading Christians on the level of fundamental faith issues, or is it a natural evolution of Christianity in a first-world nation in the twenty-first century? The central concerns of both mainstream Christianity and New Age spirituality for health, wholeness, and harmony seem to point to greater similarities than dissimilarities in many of the practices. If nothing else, raising awareness of what one does and what the practices mean to the individual engaged in them may result in fruitful conversations of faith for many involved in ministry to the sick.

Finally, beyond the boundary of the Anointing of the Sick is the consideration of rites for the dying that raises new and disturbing questions. The central and delicate balance at the heart of so much of the Anoint-

ing of the Sick was to clarify for whom the rite was designed (the seriously sick, not the dying), while at the same time trying to articulate who
was sick enough for the sacrament (the seriously sick, not just any sick).
Into the midst of that discussion comes the growing reality of the modern way people die in intensive care units, lingering longer and perhaps
more conscious of being in the dying process, surrounded by loved ones
who want desperately to do something that will help, and ultimately
knowing that their dying family member will be unable to receive Viaticum as the sacrament of the dying. All of these elements coincide with
a heightened cultural and spiritual sensitivity to the importance of ritual.
In addition, the recognition that words are often not enough or even the
most appropriate engagement for a dying person makes the sense of
touch as the last connection to those gathered around even more important. How will the changing world of medical technology and cultural
ideas of appropriate spirituality and ritual challenge, prod, or confirm the
rites for the sick? Much in the rites remains solidly helpful and life-giving, and much work remains to continue the constant adaptations and
reflections that keep the rites as living liturgy for the next generation.

Notes, Chapter Four

[1] Howard Clark Kee, *Medicine, Miracle and Magic in New Testament Times*
(Cambridge: Cambridge University Press, 1986) 12–16.

[2] Ibid., 19.

[3] Ibid., 20.

[4] Ibid.

[5] Ibid., 28.

[6] The spiritual dimension of the ancient Greek tradition has been obscured by
our knowledge of Hippocrates gained through Galen and by the use of Hippocrates during the Enlightenment. The bias of both histories may have omitted
what more recent scholarship proposes, that Hippocrates saw his work as both
medical skill and priestly ministry. The founding of the medical school of Cos by
Hippocrates in close proximity to the shrine of Asklepios suggests the presumed
interaction of these spheres of influence. (See Kee, *Medicine, Miracle and Magic*,
ch. 2.)

[7] St. Basil, writing to his friend Eustathius the physician (Letter 181), cited in
Stanley Harakas, *Health and Medicine in the Eastern Orthodox Tradition* (New
York: Crossroad, 1990) 28–29.

[8] Caesarius of Arles, Sermon 184, 5 (ed. Morin), cited in Antoine Chavasse, *Etude sur l'onction des infirmes dans l'Eglise latine du IIIe au Xie siècle* (Lyon: Librairie du Sacré-Coeur, 1942) 103–04.

[9] Peter Brown, "Relics and Social Status in the Age of Gregory of Tours," *Society and the Holy in Late Antiquity* (Berkeley: University of California Press, 1982) 232.

[10] The most comprehensive studies of the historical relationship between medicine and theology are the work of German scholars such as Heinrich Pompey, *Die Bedeutung der Medizin fur die kirchliche Seelsorge in Selbstverstandnis der sogenannten Pastoralmedizin: Eine bibliographisch-historische Untersuchung bis zur Mitte des 19. Jahrhunderts* (Fribourg: Herder, 1968), and Albert Niedermeyer, *Allgemeine Pastoralmedizin*, 2 vols. (Vienna: Herder, 1955).

[11] David F. Kelly, *The Emergence of Roman Catholic Medical Ethics in North America: An Historical-Methodological-Biographical Study* (New York: The Edwin Mellen Press, 1979) 51. Kelly's book is a fine overview of the historical development of the field from the perspective of ethics.

[12] Ibid., 52–53.

[13] Ibid.

[14] Ibid., 55.

[15] Ibid., 57.

[16] Ibid., 65–68.

[17] Ibid., 67.

[18] Angelo Scotti, *Catechismo medico* (1821), cited in Kelly, *The Emergence of Roman Catholic Medical Ethics in North America*, 67.

[19] Ibid.

[20] "By the 1920s, Catholic women religious were managing over 600 general hospitals, and the Catholic Church had become the nation's largest private healthcare provider" (Kathleen M. Joyce, "Medicine, Markets, and Morals: Catholic Hospitals and the Ethics of Abortion in Early 20th-Century America," *Working Paper Series*, Cushwa Center for the Study of American Catholicism [South Bend: University of Notre Dame, 1997] 3). The reality of the Catholic hospital network also gave rise to guilds for Catholic doctors, such as the 1932 Federation of Catholic Physicians and their journal, *Linacre Quarterly*, as well as the Catholic Hospital Association (CHA), which worked to present a unified Catholic ethical stand and overcome the squabbles between diocesan and order hospitals. The latter is traced in Robert J. Shanahan, *The History of the Catholic Hospital Association, 1915–1965* (St. Louis: Catholic Hospital Association, 1965) 30.

[21] Ibid., 11. The reality was, as Joyce says, that "the lines were not quite so sharply drawn. The people engaged in debate did not divide into two distinct, unified groups, with doctors claiming one side of the stage and all Catholics, lay and clergy, filing into place on the other side. Indeed, some doctors were themselves Catholic, and their views on therapeutic abortion were not necessarily consistent with their church's position."

[22] (New York: Joseph F. Wager, 1905) 238–39, cited in Kathleen Joyce, "Medicine, Market, and Morals," 15–16.

[23] (Philadelphia: F. A. Davis, 1946) 147–48.

[24] Ibid.,115, cited and quoted in Kelly, *Roman Catholic Medical Ethics,* 351.

[25] A 1994 American Academy of Religion address proposed that some early Roman Catholic pastoral theologians had argued against painkillers for women in labor on the grounds that the pain was their "punishment" for sin (following the Genesis address to Eve) and should be endured. This is actually a gross misrepresentation of Austin O'Malley's argument against "twilight sleep." In light of a number of test results and stillbirths, he was primarily concerned about the side effects of morphine and other drugs on the unborn child. See *The Ethics of Medical Homicide and Mutilation* (New York: The Devin–Adair Co., 1919) 232–44.

[26] Among the many studies and resources are Jeff Levin, *God, Faith and Health: Exploring the Spirituality–Healing Connection* (New York: John W. Long & Sons, Inc., 2001); *Caring and Curing: Health and Medicine in the Western Religious Traditions,* ed. Ronald L. Numbers and Darrel W. Amundsen (New York: Macmillan Publishing Co., 1986); *Health and Faith: Medical, Psychological and Religious Dimensions,* ed. John T. Chirban (New York: University Press of America, 1991); Harold G. Koenig, *The Healing Power of Faith: Science Explores Medicine's Last Great Frontier* (New York: Simon & Schuster, 1999); Harold G. Koenig, *Is Religion Good for Your Health?: The Effects of Religion on Physical and Mental Health* (London: The Haworth Press, 1997); Bruce G. Epperly, *Spirituality & Health* (Mystic, CT: Twenty-Third Publications., 1997); *Theological Roots of Wholistic Health Care,* ed. Granger E. Westberg (Hinsdale, IL: Wholistic Health Centers, Inc., 1979); *Theological Analyses of the Clinical Encounter,* ed. Gerald P. McKenny and Jonathan R. Sande (Dordrecht: Kluwer Academic Pub., 1994); *Dialogue in Medicine and Theology,* ed. Dale White (Nashville: Abingdon Press, 1967).

[27] *Faith, Spirituality and Medicine: Toward the Making of the Healing Practitioner* (New York: The Haworth Press, Inc., 2000) xiii.

[28] Ibid., 3.

[29] Paul J. Philibert, "Transitions in the Meaning of Health and Health Care: A First-World Perspective," *Illness and Healing: Concilium* 1988/5, ed. Louis-Marie Chauvet and Miklos Tomka (London: SCM Press, 1998) 3.

[30] Ibid., 6–7.

[31] King, *Faith, Spirituality and Medicine,* 2–3.

[32] Ibid., 4.

[33] Ibid., 6.

[34] Ibid., 7. It should be noted that the inexact nature of the studies claiming physical benefits for spiritual interests has raised concern among a number of physicians.

[35] This is Jeff Levin's phrase, where because "epidemiology is the study of factors that promote health and prevent illness," then religious practice and faith that contribute to the maintenance of health are categories of health prevention (*God, Faith and Health,* 7).

[36] King, *Faith, Spirituality and Medicine,* 9–10.

[37] "Chaplains and Pastoral Services," ch. 8 in *Faith, Spirituality and Medicine,* even lists the sample curriculum and requirements of CPE as a reassurance to professional health workers that they are working with "experts"! See especially pp. 73–81.

[38] Ibid., 42.

[39] However, recent diocesan pastoral letters such as that of Bishop Grahmann of Dallas have begun to address this: "Today's Pastoral Ministry to the Sick and Dying," *Origins* 32:31 (January 2003) 513–15.

[40] The foreword says, "The revised and expanded text of the *Ethical and Religious Directives for Catholic Health Care Services* (Washington, D.C.: USCC, 1995) was developed by the Committee on Doctrine of the National Conference of Catholic Bishops and approved as the national code by the full body of bishops at their November 1994 General Meeting. These *Directives* have been recommended for implementation by the diocesan bishop and are authorized for publication by the undersigned" (namely, Monsignor Robert N. Lynch, General Secretary).

[41] Ibid., 1.

[42] Ibid.

[43] Ibid., 5.

[44] Ibid., 13.

[45] Ibid., 10.

[46] Ibid.

[47] Ibid.

[48] Paul Philibert, "Transitions in the Meaning of Health and Health Care: A First-World Perspective," 6.

[49] For examples of general surveys see David Spangler, *The New Age Vision* (Forres: Findhorn Publications, 1980), and Paul Heelas, *The New Age Movement. The Celebration of the Self and the Sacralization of Modernity* (Oxford: Blackwell, 1996).

[50] John Paul II's address to the bishops of Iowa, Kansas, Missouri, and Nebraska on May 28, 1993.

[51] Pontifical Councils for Culture and Interreligious Dialogue, "Jesus Christ, the Bearer of the Water of Life: A Christian Reflection on the New Age," *Origins* 32:35 (February 13, 2003). The foreword describes the study as "a provisional report. It is the fruit of the common reflection of the Working Group on New Religious Movements, composed of staff members of different dicasteries of the Holy See: the pontifical councils for Culture and for Interreligious Dialogue (which are the principal redactors for this project), the Congregation for the Evangelization of Peoples, and the Pontifical Council for Promoting Christian Unity" (pp. 570–71). The following references use the pagination of this edition.

[52] As with most documents written by committees, the internal cohesion is sometimes lacking. There are attacks on fairly innocuous practices such as the use of the enneagram (573), implications that stewardship for the creation and ecology may be anti-Christian (578), and odd jabs at the venerable Christian doctrine of divinization (578, 583), but these are mixed in with thoughtful self-reflection and a fair discernment of what constitutes inculturation and what constitutes concerns of misleading syncretism.

[53] Ibid., 571.

[54] Ibid.

[55] Ibid., 572.

[56] John Paul II, *Acta Apostolicae Sedis* 86/4, 330, cited in "Jesus Christ, the Bearer of the Water of Life," 571.

[57] Ibid., 584.

[58] Ibid., 572.

[59] Ibid., 573.

[60] Ibid., 574.

[61] New Age has "a goal of superseding or transcending particular religions in order to create space for a universal religion which could unite humanity" (ibid., 581).

[62] The clearest articulation of this fundamental American sense of the "subjectification of reality" is by M. Francis Mannion, in his article "Liturgy and the Present Crisis of Culture," *Worship* 62 (1988) 98–123. There he articulates the conflict between an insidious cultural sense that there is no greater reality than "I" and a religious system such as Christianity that is predicated on the greater reality of "we."

[63] Paul Heelas, *The New Age Movement,* 173ff., cited in "Jesus Christ, the Bearer of the Water of Life," 579.

[64] "Jesus Christ, the Bearer of the Water of Life," 580.

[65] Philip Jenkins, *The Next Christendom: The Coming of Global Christianity* (Oxford: Oxford University Press, 2002) 77.

[66] The amount of secondary writing stressing wholeness as a primary effect of the sacrament of anointing is in inverse proportion to its actual presence in the rite, to the extent that the secondary writing begins to appear as wishful thinking or prophetic encouragement. In the doctrinal texts, concern "for the whole person" (PCS 4) stands alone in the General Introduction and the Introduction to the Anointing of the Sick. In the liturgical texts several prayers for "full health" (such as PCS 125B) could certainly be interpreted as a prayer for wholeness. Clearer are "we pray that the sick may be restored to health by the gift of his mercy and made whole in his fullness" (PCS 135A) as well as "heal the afflicted and make them whole" (PCS 146A). Most notable of the secondary literature are two key texts: Charles W. Gusmer, *And You Visited Me: Sacramental Ministry to the Sick and the Dying* (New York: Pueblo Pub. Co., 1989) 139–45, and David N. Power, "The Sacrament of Anointing: Open Questions," *The Pastoral Care of the Sick,* ed. Mary Collins and David N. Power (London: SCM Press, 1991) 103–04.

[67] Jenkins, *The Next Christendom,* 136.

[68] Ibid.,130.

[69] Ibid.,125–27.

[70] "Jesus Christ, the Bearer of the Water of Life," 574.

[71] Ibid., 575.

[72] Ibid.

[73] Ibid.

[74] Ibid., 582.

[75] See the articulation of the qualities of inculturation in Anscar Chupungco, *Liturgical Inculturation: Sacramentals, Religiosity, and Catechesis* (Collegeville: Liturgical Press, 1992) especially "A Definition of Terms" in ch. 1.

[76] "Jesus Christ, the Bearer of the Water of Life," 573.

[77] Kristiaan Depoortere, "You Have Striven with God (Genesis 32:28): A Pastoral-Theological Reflection on the Image of God and Suffering," *God and Human*

Suffering, ed. Jan Lambrecht and Raymond F. Collins (Louv[a] 1990) 213. Depoortere quotes M. Pijnenburg, "Levensbe[s] pleegkundige zorg," *Metamedica* 64 (1985) 272–73.

[78] Daniel J. Louw, *Meaning in Suffering: A Theological Reflec[the Resurrection for Pastoral Care and Counseling* (Frankfurt: Pe[...

[79] Joseph A. Selling, "Moral Questioning and Human Suffering: In Search of a Credible Response to the Meaning of Suffering," *God and Human Suffering,* 157.

[80] Ibid., 164.

[81] Lucien Richard, *What Are They Saying about the Theology of Suffering?* (New York: Paulist Press, 1992) 10.

[82] Christopher Lash, *The Culture of Narcissism* (London: Abacus, 1980) 36–41.

[83] Lucien Richard, *What Are They Saying about the Theology of Suffering?,* 10.

[84] "The minister should take into account the particular circumstances, needs, and desires of the sick and of other members of the faithful and should willingly use the various opportunities that the rites provide" (PCS 40).

[85] Cor Traets, "The Sick and Suffering Person: A Liturgical/Sacramental Approach," *God and Human Suffering,* 190. Traets quotes from "the 'Pastoral Considerations'" of the Flemish Rite, based on the same French translation and arrangement as the American rite's structure.

[86] Joseph A. Selling, "Moral Questioning and Human Suffering," 168.

[87] The Flemish translation of the Ritual has the representational quality of the gathered family and friends quite clearly included: "Lord Jesus . . . let him/her recognize your love in our care and encouragement" (Cor Traets, "The Sick and Suffering Person," 198).

[88] It would also seem to be consistent with the foundational text of James 5, particularly in the continuation of the passage through verse 16: "Therefore confess your sins to one another, and pray for one another, so that you may be healed."

[89] Selling, "Moral Questioning and Human Suffering," 156.

[90] Cited in Richard, *What Are They Saying about the Theology of Suffering?,* 24. Ch. 2 is an exploration of Schillebeeckx's theology: "God and Suffering: Edward Schillebeeckx."

[91] Louw, *Meaning in Suffering,* 28–37.

[92] *The Oxford Bible Commentary,* ed. John Barton and John Muddinan (Oxford: Oxford University Press, 2001) 1195.

[93] Ibid.

[94] *New Jerome Biblical Commentary,* ed. Raymond Brown (New Jersey: Prentice Hall, 1990).

[95] "Absolutely speaking the genitive in 'the sufferings of Christ' can be objective (sufferings borne for Christ), qualitative (sufferings like those of Christ), subjective (sufferings undergone by Christ), or mystical (sufferings undergone by members of Christ's body)," *New Catholic Commentary* (London: Thomas Nelson & Sons, Ltd., 1969) 1201.

[96] *Eerdmans Bible Commentary,* ed. D. Guthrie and J. A. Motyer (Grand Rapids, MI: Eerdmans, 1970) 1145.

[97] Frederick S Paxton, *Christianizing Death: The Creation of a Ritual Process in Early Medieval Europe* (Ithaca: Cornell University Press, 1990) 39.

[98] Of the many descriptions of martyrs' deaths conforming to Christ's death, perhaps the death of Blandina best exemplifies dying in Christ: "After being tossed a good deal by the animal, she no longer perceived what was happening because of the hope and possession of all she believed in and because of her intimacy with Christ. Thus she too was offered in sacrifice, while the pagans themselves admitted that no woman had ever suffered so much in their experience" (The Martyrs of Lyon," *The Acts of the Christian Martyrs,* trans. and ed. Herbert Musurillo [Oxford: Clarendon Press, 1972] 79–81).

[99] Edward Schillebeeckx, *Christ: The Experience of Jesus as Lord* (New York: Crossroad, 1980) 821, cited in Richard, *What Are They Saying about the Theology of Suffering?*, 29.

[100] Selling, "Moral Questioning and Human Suffering," 170.

[101] *Lumen Gentium* 11. The revised edition of *Pastoral Care of the Sick* now cites the correct paragraph from the Dogmatic Constitution on the Church.

[102] "Allowing context to create interpretation is fundamentally a passive response to the phenomenon of human suffering. When this passivity is allowed to function in the extreme, it may even lead to a certain fascination with suffering itself." Joseph A. Selling develops the contrast between this passive acceptance and active interpretation in his essay on "Moral Questioning and Human Suffering," 168–75.

[103] Ibid., 176.

[104] Traets, "The Sick and Suffering Person," 206.

[105] Schillebeeckx, *Christ: The Experience of Jesus as Lord,* 640.

[106] In his paper on suffering, John Paul II traces this love through the union of our suffering with Christ's: "In the cross of Christ not only is the redemption accomplished through suffering, but also human suffering itself has been redeemed . . . in bringing about the redemption through suffering, Christ has also raised human suffering to the level of the redemption. Thus each man in his suffering can also become a sharer in the redemptive suffering of Christ" (*Salvifici Doloris*, 19: AAS 76 [1984] 212).

[107] Richard, *What Are They Saying about the Theology of Suffering?*, 34, in which he cites Schllebeeckx, *Christ*, 820.

[108] See Lizette Larson-Miller, "The Church's Pastoral Care of the Sick," *Ministry and Liturgy* 30 (2003) 15, and Elaine Ramshaw, *Ritual and Pastoral Care* (Philadelphia: Fortress Press, 1987) especially ch. 1.

[109] The bishops of Belgium, *Geloofsboek* (Tielt, 1987) 118–21. Cor Traets cites this quote from the rite in his "The Sick and Suffering Person," 184.

[110] Ibid.,195. He references Henri Denis, "Quand meurt l'extreme-onction. Essai sur le renouveau de l'onction des maladies," *Lumiere et Vie* 138 (1978) 67–79, and F. Isambert, *Rite et efficacité symbolique: Rites et symbols;* 8 (Paris: editions du Cerf, 1979) ch. IV.

[111] " . . . just a little ill-will is enough to point out that the word 'death' occurs in the order of service for the anointing of a sick person only with reference to

Christ" (Kristiaan Depoortere, "Recent Developments in the Anointing of the Sick," 96).

[112] In the anecdotal written responses to the 1994 NACC Survey, 174 respondents "addressed the use of and need for alternative rituals to minimize problems associated with their inability to locate a priest to anoint patients. 70 respondents stated that as chaplains, women religious, and non-Catholic ministers, they have at one time or another anointed a patient. They have heard confessions (especially for dying patients), designed alternative anointing rituals or ceremonies, improvised . . . ." Particularly in emergency situations (trauma unit or other) these alternative rituals were deemed necessary and "acceptable": "Survey Results: Analysis of Written Comments," *Survey on the Sacrament of the Anointing of the Sick,* NACC (February 1995) 6.

[113] One of the most perplexing has been Gisbert Greshake, "The Anointing of the Sick: The Oscillation of the Church between Physical and Spiritual Healing," *Illness and Healing,* 81–87. He presents an either/or situation with no explicit sense that it should be and is probably both/and. Either one stresses the "first pole: anointing the sick" as in Scripture and the New Testament, or the "second pole: extreme unction" as with the wisdom of the scholastic period. These are contrasted as an obsession with physical healing (first pole) in which the individual rituals (national adaptations) "go one step further in their practical instructions; influenced by some historians of liturgy with their extremely one-sided view of the practice of anointing in the early church . . . they emphasize the 'medicinal' character of the sacrament, relate it to any form of illness, and thus seek to detach it completely from the dimensions 'in the face of death.'" Or the anointing for the dying, extreme unction, which was the sacrament when the sacrament was named thus ("What is the hermeneutical significance of the fact that in the rise of a specific theology of the sacraments, the fifth sacrament was counted among the seven sacraments not as the anointing of the sick but as Extreme Unction, and as such constituted the sacramental 'cosmos', i.e., the ordering between the sacraments and their relationship to human life?"). For a further reflection on Greshake's ecclesial and theological perspective, see Lambert Leussen, "L'Interpretation du sacrament de l'onction des maladies dans le contexte d'une société sécularisée. La position de Gisbert Greshake," *Questions Liturgiques* 74 (1993) 191–201.

[114] Depoortere, "Recent Developments in the Anointing of the Sick," 93.

[115] Ibid., 96.

[116] Ibid., 97.

[117] Ibid.

[118] Touch and hearing are generally understood to be the last senses that remain with us when we are dying, hence the importance of both to retain a connection between the dying person and those journeying with the dying person. For a wonderful description of the importance of touch, see Megory Anderson, *Sacred Dying: Creating Rituals for Embracing the End of Life* (Roseville, CA: Prima Publishing, 2001) 151–59.

[119] Alone of the ecumenical rites found in highly liturgical churches, the Episcopal rites for the sick have added a ritual at the removing of life support and a

prayer for those who would wish to receive communion but are not able to do so *(Enriching Our Worship II)*. Some ecumenical cooperation along the lines of reflection and experience in these adaptations would be helpful in order to share what both works and what does not stand the test of time.

Conclusion

For anyone who ministers as a hospital chaplain or has done a required round of Clinical Pastoral Education (CPE) in a hospital setting, remembering the experience of being woken in the middle of the night can bring to mind a variety of emotions. Sometimes the feeling was annoyance, but most often it was dread, or fear, or feelings of inadequacy, and always a *memento mori,* a reminder of one's own eventual death. Most hospital deaths occur at night, and while not every chaplain call is for a death, the reality is that it is often an impending death or a frightened patient for whom the quiet of the night opens up time for reflection on the fragility of life. I have spent many hours of the night sitting with a dying patient and their family members or friends, grateful for a Catholic upbringing that gave me the tools of ritual gestures, memorized psalms, prayers, litanies, and rosaries to assist in all-night vigils with the sick and dying, and to offer a type of presence and activity that could engage others with a minimum of preparation. The *Pastoral Care of the Sick: Rites of Anointing and Viaticum* is an invaluable collection of resources to assist in visiting the sick or the dying Christian, but the contents are ultimately tools that must be wisely adapted to each situation. Ritual books, ritual texts, and ritual actions must always serve the gathering of the Body of Christ manifested in the loving presence of its members. Whether it is a gathering of two or of two hundred, the first ministry is one of presence, of attentiveness, of listening, and of representation. Showing up and being there in prayer are the basic rituals; the others are helpful, and the sacramental actions both life-giving and comforting when available. In other words, the wealth of resources for the Church's ministry with the sick and dying is both a blessing in its abundance and a danger in that those resources have the potential to get in the way of real human interactions, which are the basis for our human understanding of our relationship with God.

The blessings of Pastoral Care of the Sick were made apparent to me the first time I taught a graduate course on rites for the sick and dying in an ecumenical setting. It was fascinating to hear from a number of students from free church traditions who looked with some envy on the resources of PCS and those of other liturgical churches. One student summed it up well when he said, "it is hard to lead spontaneous prayer for five straight hours; I wish we had something like this too!" In the introduction of this book, the PCS was lauded for both its attention to breadth of care and depth of sacramental focus. The breadth of resources in PCS allows for the sustained and ongoing ministry to the sick, especially when an illness lasts for months or even years, but it also facilitates the all too common experience of journeying with a dying Christian through the hours of the night, hours in which silent prayer and exhaustion are punctuated with the texts and ritual actions from the PCS.

This study, however, has been primarily concerned with the sacramental core of the PCS, namely the sacrament of the anointing of the sick. And while ritually and theologically the sacrament is situated in the middle of the whole spectrum of rituals, the experience of many sick Christians is that the anointing of the sick is often done without the sustained context of care for the sick (or that sustained care and rituals for the sick do not lead into the anointing of the sick). In other words, the sacramental action of anointing often has to stand on its own as the expression of the Church's care of the sick and the abiding presence and comfort of Christ. How well it does that is ultimately impossible to discern. As mentioned in the chapters above, there has been a rather thorough acceptance of the new rite (the new rite for the sick as opposed to extreme unction and its association with the last rites). But often that acceptance is in addition to, not instead of, "last rites." In other words, many hospital chaplains (and parish priests) are summoned to give the last rites to a dying Christian, even when the family members are catechized into the experience of anointing the sick and/or communal rites of anointing in their own parishes. The popular association of the need for ritual actions and for forgiveness of sins at the time of death lives on in the minds of many Christians, including many non-Roman Catholic Christians who also request that these rites be done. And while the details of what is involved in so-called "last rites" in a post-Vatican II Church are fuzzy for some, the sacraments of reconciliation and anointing are usually what many people have in mind when they make the request.

But the anointing of the sick has gained great acceptance in addition to and separate from the desire for these last rites. In some parts of the United States, the communal anointings in parishes have exemplified the continuity of the sacramental core of the Church's care for the sick with all the other rituals of the sick. It is often in these communities that a vibrant and engaging ministry to the sick by many members of the parish leads into and flows out of the communal anointings, allowing for the breadth of care that the designers of PCS must have had in mind. In a number of parishes, deaneries, or dioceses, personal experience with PCS has evolved into a parish-based care for the sick in which parishioners prepare to be chaplains to members of their own parish working in conjunction with parish-based nurses. In the more frequent experience of individual anointings, whether in hospitals, in rest homes, in hospices, or in domestic settings, it is the depth of the sacramental encounter that takes precedence. The human medium of the sacramental encounter is always more ambiguous, however, and how well the sick person is cared for and how effectively the love and compassion of God is manifested through the one anointing will always vary.

It was a delight to work in a hospital setting with two wonderful priests who left in their wake hallways of patients whose request for a visit, for communion, for confession, or for anointing was responded to with compassion, with presence, and with genuine care and careful ritual. It is also encouraging to know that many seminaries have taken seriously the need to teach both pastoral care and liturgy and the rituals in which those two arenas intersect. To engage the necessary skills for good ritual and the necessary skills for good pastoral care is not easy. These various skills often find a home in different personality types, but we demand that they be present in a single individual in doing this sacramental rite as well as other rites. The least we can do is choose with care the people who will be doing these important ministries and train them to the best of our ability. But the reality of a priest shortage, more acute in some geographical parts of the country than in others, impacts all sacramental encounters, and the surveys and studies of groups such as those advocating for more extensive ministerial responsibilities for permanent deacons and for certified hospital chaplains point to the situation in which many caregivers find themselves today, namely that the restriction of anointing of the sick to priests alone often means that their loved ones cannot be anointed sacramentally. If both the trend toward a reduction in the number of ordained priests continues, as well as the restriction to priests as proper ministers of the anointing of the sick, the other pastoral issues surrounding the sacrament become moot, and the pastoral care of the sick through other forms and rituals will need to grow and take precedence.

In spite of the pastoral challenges in the doing of the sacrament, the theological reflection on the meaning of suffering, sickness, dying, health, the Church's ministry, and many other issues surrounding all pastoral care of the sick, continue. And the reflections continue in two different arenas as noted in Chapters Three and Four above. They continue first within the Church, articulating how the experience of sickness gives rise to new understandings of our participation in Christ, and what the role of the Church is at turning points in a person's life. The sacrament of the anointing of the sick in its present form is now thirty years-old, twenty years-old in the English language edition. How it has changed the views of Catholic Christians towards their own bodies, towards health and sickness, towards their own ability to minister and bring the presence of Christ to others should be the focus of a new and wide-ranging survey, like those we have had in the past concerning parish life and particularly participation in the Eucharist.

The arena in which theological reflection takes place is widening because of an increasingly pluralistic world and the role that the Church and individual Christians play in the world. Pastoral care of the sick is both a countercultural statement of faith and an avenue of inculturated missiology with much potential for growth. During a time of stories and remembrances of the deceased at the recent funeral of a Christian friend who died in a Zen hospice in San Francisco, one story stood out. It was the story of how seriously he took his role as the representative of Christianity in the hospice and how important it was to him to manifest all that was good about Christian prayer, Christian ritual, the sacrament of anointing, and Viaticum—all in a non-Christian setting. The evangelization was not one of words but of ritual engagement, and it apparently made an impact on a number of non-Christians (or former Christians) who assumed that Christianity only talked but never really did anything. That is one way of being Church in the world; another way is by the institutional and personal interchange between the arenas described in Chapter Four, such as spirituality and health care, or spirituality and culture. What will the next typical edition of the sacrament of the anointing of the sick look like? How will changes in health care, the experience of living through illness and the experience of dying in the United States impact the next version of the rites? How will cultural assumptions about spirituality, life after death, the importance of the body and what makes up a human being change the liturgy? How will widespread epidemics and/or the eradication of life-threatening diseases change our perception of the need for anointing of the sick?

Less speculative and futuristic questions might be directed toward some present ritual realities such as how the experience of weekly massage therapy in hospice settings changes people's perceptions of the anointing of the sick, or how the impact of the anointing of the sick is changed in light of non-sacramental anointings. Other questions remain as to how we address viaticum and the sacrament of the dying when life-support systems prevent its reception. More theological concerns might be summarized by the growing concern that New Age spirituality has on people's perceptions of health and sickness, and what the relationship of personal and corporate sin is to sickness. Contemporary technical advances in health care raise for us the dilemma of articulating what we believe about life and when it ends. How do we disconnect life-support? When does someone actually die? And how do we respond to that in prayer and ritual?

These are only a few of the many questions that continue to be raised from within and from beyond the experiences of the Church with regard to sickness and health. The sacrament of the anointing of the sick cannot address all of the emerging issues, but by its very continuity within the longer tradition of the Church and by its faithfulness to the tradition of Jesus' own care for the sick and the writings of the early Christians, it offers a starting and ending place when confronted with sickness and death, allowing us to pray with the sick through the words of the final blessing, that God the Father will bless us, that God the Son will heal us, and that God the Holy Spirit will enlighten us unto health and salvation.

Index of Documents

Index of Scripture References

Index of Proper Names

Index of Subjects